Blooming™ Category Activities

Janet R. Lanza
Lynn K. Flahive

Skills: Categorization, Vocabulary, Thinking
Age Level: 3 thru 8
Grades: Preschool thru 3

LinguiSystems, Inc.
3100 4th Avenue
East Moline, IL 61244-9700
800-776-4332

FAX: 800-577-4555
E-mail: service@linguisystems.com
Web: linguisystems.com

© 2006 LinguiSystems, Inc.

Printed in the U.S.A.

ISBN 0-7606-0654-4

About the Authors

Janet R. Lanza, M.S., CCC-SLP, has worked as a speech-language pathologist in public schools, private practice, and a university clinic in Texas since 1976. She has been on the faculty of the Department of Communication Sciences and Disorders at Texas Christian University in Fort Worth, Texas, since 1989. At the TCU Miller Speech and Hearing Clinic, Janet is an instructor and clinical supervisor for classroom settings of preschool children with a variety of communication disorders.

Lynn K. Flahive, M.S., CCC-SLP, is a Board Recognized Specialist in Child Language with over 25 years experience as a speech-language pathologist. She worked in public and private schools in Wisconsin, Ohio, Illinois, and Texas for 12 years before joining the Department of Communication Sciences and Disorders at Texas Christian University in Fort Worth, TX. She has special interest in working with preschoolers and early elementary-aged children with phonological disorders and/or language delays. She provides workshops at the state and national levels on these topics as well as publishing materials with LinguiSystems. Additionally, Lynn served as the Executive Director of the National Students Speech Language Hearing Association for six years and is the current past president of the Texas Speech-Language-Hearing Association.

Dedication

We dedicate this book to our editor, Karen Stontz. It has been our pleasure to work with Karen on several LinguiSystems products. She is a true professional who makes our job easy. Thanks, Karen, for all you've done!

Illustrations by Margaret Warner
Cover design by Chris Claus
Edited by Karen Stontz
Page layout by Christine Buysse

Table of Contents

Introduction 7

Food
Project 9
Picture Cards 10
Family Letter 13
Activities 14
Worksheet 15
Concepts 16
Bloom's Taxonomy 19

Animals
Project 20
Picture Cards 21
Family Letter 24
Activities 25
Worksheet 26
Concepts 28
Bloom's Taxonomy 31

Body Parts
Project 32
Picture Cards 33
Family Letter 36
Activities 37
Worksheet 38
Concepts 39
Bloom's Taxonomy 42

Clothing
Project 43
Picture Cards 44
Family Letter 47
Activities 48
Worksheet 49
Concepts 51
Bloom's Taxonomy 53

Around the Home
Project 54
Picture Cards 55
Family Letter 58
Activities 59
Worksheet 60
Concepts 62
Bloom's Taxonomy 65

Table of Contents, continued

Day and Night
Project 66
Picture Cards 67
Family Letter 70
Activities 71
Worksheet 72
Concepts 73
Bloom's Taxonomy 75

Occupations
Project 76
Picture Cards 77
Family Letter 80
Activities 81
Worksheet 82
Concepts 83
Bloom's Taxonomy 85

Transportation
Project 86
Picture Cards 87
Family Letter 90
Activities 91
Worksheet 92
Concepts 93
Bloom's Taxonomy 95

Toys
Project 96
Picture Cards 97
Family Letter 100
Activities 101
Worksheet 102
Concepts 103
Bloom's Taxonomy 106

Sports
Project 107
Picture Cards 108
Family Letter 111
Activities 112
Worksheet 113
Concepts 114
Bloom's Taxonomy 116

Table of Contents, continued

School
Project 117
Picture Cards 118
Family Letter 121
Activities 122
Worksheet 123
Concepts 125
Bloom's Taxonomy 128

Holidays
Project 129
Picture Cards 130
Family Letter 133
Activities 134
Worksheet 135
Concepts 137
Bloom's Taxonomy 138

Plants and Trees
Project 139
Picture Cards 140
Family Letter 143
Activities 144
Worksheet 145
Concepts 147
Bloom's Taxonomy 149

Ocean and Beach
Project 150
Picture Cards 151
Family Letter 154
Activities 155
Worksheet 156
Concepts 158
Bloom's Taxonomy 159

Musical Instruments
Project 160
Picture Cards 161
Family Letter 164
Activities 165
Worksheet 166
Concepts 168
Bloom's Taxonomy 169

Table of Contents, continued

Seasons and Weather
Project 170
Picture Cards 172
Family Letter 175
Activities 176
Worksheet 177
Concepts 178
Bloom's Taxonomy 179

Bugs and Insects
Project 180
Picture Cards 181
Family Letter 184
Activities 185
Worksheet 186
Concepts 188
Bloom's Taxonomy 190

Introduction

The materials in *Blooming Category Activities* are based on interactive lessons, vocabulary development, and *Bloom's Taxonomy of Educational Objectives*. Their purposes are to help children grow their word knowledge based on categories, to promote conversational teaching and learning, and to expand thinking skills. *Blooming Category Activities* can be used with individuals and is also especially effective for use with groups.

Blooming Category Activities consists of seventeen units based on the vocabulary in age-appropriate categories. Each unit is chock-full of hands-on, interactive activities designed to make learning meaningful and fun. The pages in this book are not meant for drill, but as guides to elicit the desired targets in a natural, enjoyable fashion.

The seventeen categorical units in *Blooming Category Activities* are these:

- Food
- Animals
- Body Parts
- Clothes
- Day and Night
- Around the House
- Occupations
- Transportation
- Toys
- Sports
- School
- Holidays
- Plants and Trees
- Ocean and Beach
- Musical Instruments
- Seasons and Weather
- Bugs and Insects

Major Components of Each Unit

Project
Each unit begins with a page that describes and pictures a project, craft, or role-play. Some of the components in the unit, including many of the Bloom's Taxonomy questions, are centered on this main activity. This first page lists the materials needed for the activity as well as directions, with suggested areas of conversation.

Picture Cards
Twenty-seven cards that picture vocabulary from the targeted category are included in each unit. These picture cards may be photocopied and used for a variety of vocabulary teaching methods. Many of the ideas listed in the Activities section involve the picture cards.

Family Letter
A letter to the child's family accompanies each unit. This letter informs the family of the targeted category. A picture on the letter helps members of the family elicit some of the category-related vocabulary. There are also ten suggested examples of ways to use the vocabulary in the family's everyday life.

Introduction, continued

Activities
One part of each unit is a page of fun, interactive ideas for activities to elicit the targeted category-related vocabulary. Some of the suggested activities in each unit involve use of the picture cards. You may choose to do one or all of the activities and also use them as springboards for your own creative ways to teach the vocabulary.

Worksheet
Each unit contains a worksheet designed to increase receptive understanding and expressive use of the vocabulary for that unit. The worksheet is different for each lesson. It includes activities such as What's Wrong Here?, matching, associations, sequencing, following directions, and defining. The completed worksheet would be appropriate for review as home carry-over.

Concepts
The basic concept words that are so important for a child's language development are specifically targeted in category-related worksheets or crafts in each unit. Because it is most effective when concept words are taught in a variety of situations, you are encouraged to take advantage of every opportunity throughout the lessons in *Blooming Category Activities* to also target concepts.

Bloom's Taxonomy
Opportunities are given in each lesson to practice answering questions and to develop higher level thinking skills through the use of questions following the hierarchy presented in *Bloom's Taxonomy of Educational Objectives*. This hierarchy goes from the concrete Knowledge level to the more abstract levels of Analysis, Synthesis, and Evaluation. The questions for each unit center on that unit's category and many of them focus on the main project.

When using these questions, it is important that you present and discuss the vocabulary before you ask the questions. You can either ask questions from all levels of Bloom's Taxonomy or start at the lowest level and progress to the level at which the child experiences difficulty.

Through many years of experience and study, we know that our teaching is most effective and learning is most successful when activities are interactive and hands-on. Targets such as vocabulary development through the use of categories are best presented and habituated when elicited in a variety of situations. We sincerely hope that the activities and materials in this book make it easier for you to help develop your students' vocabulary and thinking skills and to have fun while accomplishing these goals.

Janet and Lynn

Food

Paper Plate Meals

Materials:
- copy of the food picture cards from this unit on pages 10-12
- glue
- three paper plates per child
- scissors

Directions:
- Place the picture cards on the table facedown in a pile.
- Write *breakfast* on one plate, *lunch* on another, and *dinner* on the third one.
- Talk about the three meals we eat, when we eat them, and the foods that we might eat at each one.
- Tell the child to pick a picture.
- Have the child name the food and tell at which meal she would eat it.
- Let the child glue the picture onto the appropriate plate.

Food

Picture Cards

Objective: The child will increase receptive understanding and expressive use of food vocabulary.

apple	banana	cake
candy	carrot	cheese
chips	cookies	corn

Unit 1
Blooming Category Activities

10

Copyright © 2006 LinguiSystems, Inc.

Food

Picture Cards, cont.

eggs	fish	French fries
grapes	green beans	hamburger
hot dog	ice cream	milk

Unit 1
Blooming Category Activities

Food

Picture Cards, cont.

orange	pancakes	peas
pie	pizza	popcorn
pretzels	sandwich	steak

Unit 1
Blooming Category Activities

12

Copyright © 2006 LinguiSystems, Inc.

Food

Family Letter

Dear Family,

In speech, we are learning about food and the vocabulary that goes with this category. You can help your child use this vocabulary at home. Talk about the picture below with your child and help her use food words to answer the questions. Then put this page on your refrigerator or by your grocery list to remind everyone to help your child talk about food. Some ideas to encourage talking about food vocabulary are at the bottom of the page.

Thank you, _____

Which meal is the family eating? Tell about the foods in your favorite meal.

- I eat **eggs** for **breakfast**.
- Please pass the **salt**.
- Let's grow **carrots** in our garden.
- What **food group** is your favorite?
- May I have an **ice-cream cone** for **dessert**?

- **Milk** belongs in the **dairy** group.
- What are you having for **lunch**?
- I like to eat **popcorn** as a **snack**.
- **Pretzels** are **salty**.
- I found the **green beans** in the **produce** section.

Unit 1
Blooming Category Activities

Food   Activities

For some of these activities, you will photocopy and cut apart the picture cards on pages 10-12.

- Cut out the picture cards and put them in a bag. Have the child pull out a picture and name the food item.

- Put various fruits and vegetables in a bag. Blindfold the child and have her pull a fruit or vegetable out of the bag. Have her describe the item by telling how it feels, using adjectives such as *smooth*, *long*, *round*, and *sticky*.

- Place empty food boxes and cans around the room. Let the child go shopping using a toy grocery basket or bag. Have the child name and describe each item she "buys."

- Have the child sort the food picture cards by categories such as *fruit*, *vegetable*, *drink*, *snack*, or *meat*.

- Have different foods for the child to sample, such as pretzels, popcorn, cereal, and pickles. Let the child describe how each item tastes, using adjectives such as *sweet*, *salty*, and *sour*.

- Dress the child as a chef and let her use pots and pans to pretend to make a meal. Be sure to talk about the verbs you use, such as *pour*, *stir*, *mix*, *serve*, and *eat*.

- Have each child tell what her favorite food is and why.

- Cut out "scoops of ice cream" from various colored sheets of construction paper. Cut out an "ice-cream cone" from brown paper. Have the child add scoops of ice cream to her cone, telling what color each scoop is. You can also use real decorations, such as candy sprinkles or chocolate chips, to decorate the scoops. Talk about where the child puts each decoration, such as *on the top*, *next to the chip*, or *on the right*.

- Let the child use empty food boxes and cans to set up a grocery store. Have her arrange the "aisle" by category. For example, she would put corn in the vegetable section, popcorn in the snack section, and cereal in the breakfast food section.

- Let the child string Froot Loops onto a length of yarn to make a bracelet or necklace. As she puts each piece of cereal on the yarn, have her tell what color it is. You can also have her count how many pieces of cereal she has on her bracelet/necklace.

- Pretend to go out to eat at a restaurant. Let one child order her meal and the other child take the order and serve the meal.

- Have the child pick two food items from the food picture cards. Then ask her to tell how the two items are the same and how they are different.

Food

Worksheet

Objective: The child will tell how two food items are the same and how they are different by answering *how* questions.

Say, "Name all of the food items in both columns. Now draw a line from a food item on the right side to a food item on the left that goes with it." After the child has made an association, ask her to tell you how the two items are the same and how they are different. For example, she might say, "An orange and orange juice are the same because they are both orange. They are different because you eat an orange, but you drink orange juice."

When the page is complete, have the child tell the process by which the item on the left becomes the item on the right.

Unit 1
Blooming Category Activities
15
Copyright © 2006 LinguiSystems, Inc.

Food

Concepts

→ **Objective**: The child will demonstrate receptive understanding and expressive use of basic concepts while completing the activity.

Place Setting

Materials:
- a sheet of construction paper, any color
- scissors
- glue

Directions:
- Explain to the child that the sheet of construction paper is now a place mat.
- Cut out the pictures on pages 17 and 18.
- Tell the child to pick a certain item.
- Using concept words, tell her where to glue the item on the place mat.
- Continue until the child has completed a place setting.

Suggested Concepts to Target:

• **center**	Glue the plate in the **center** of the paper.
• **left/right**	The napkin goes on the **left** side of the plate. The knife goes on the **right** side of the plate.
• **next to/beside**	Glue the spoon **next to** the knife. The napkin is **beside** the plate.
• **above/below**	The glass goes **above** the plate. The plate is **below** the glass.
• **first/last**	What is the **first** thing you glued on the plate? What is the **last** item you glued on the place mat?
• **between**	What is **between** the plate and the spoon?
• **on/off**	Put the fork **on** the napkin. Take the cap **off** the glue.
• **same/different**	How is your place mat the **same** as your friend's? How is your place mat **different**?
• **always/sometimes/never**	I **always** eat soup with a spoon. **Sometimes** I eat cereal with my fingers. I **never** eat ice cream with a knife.

Food

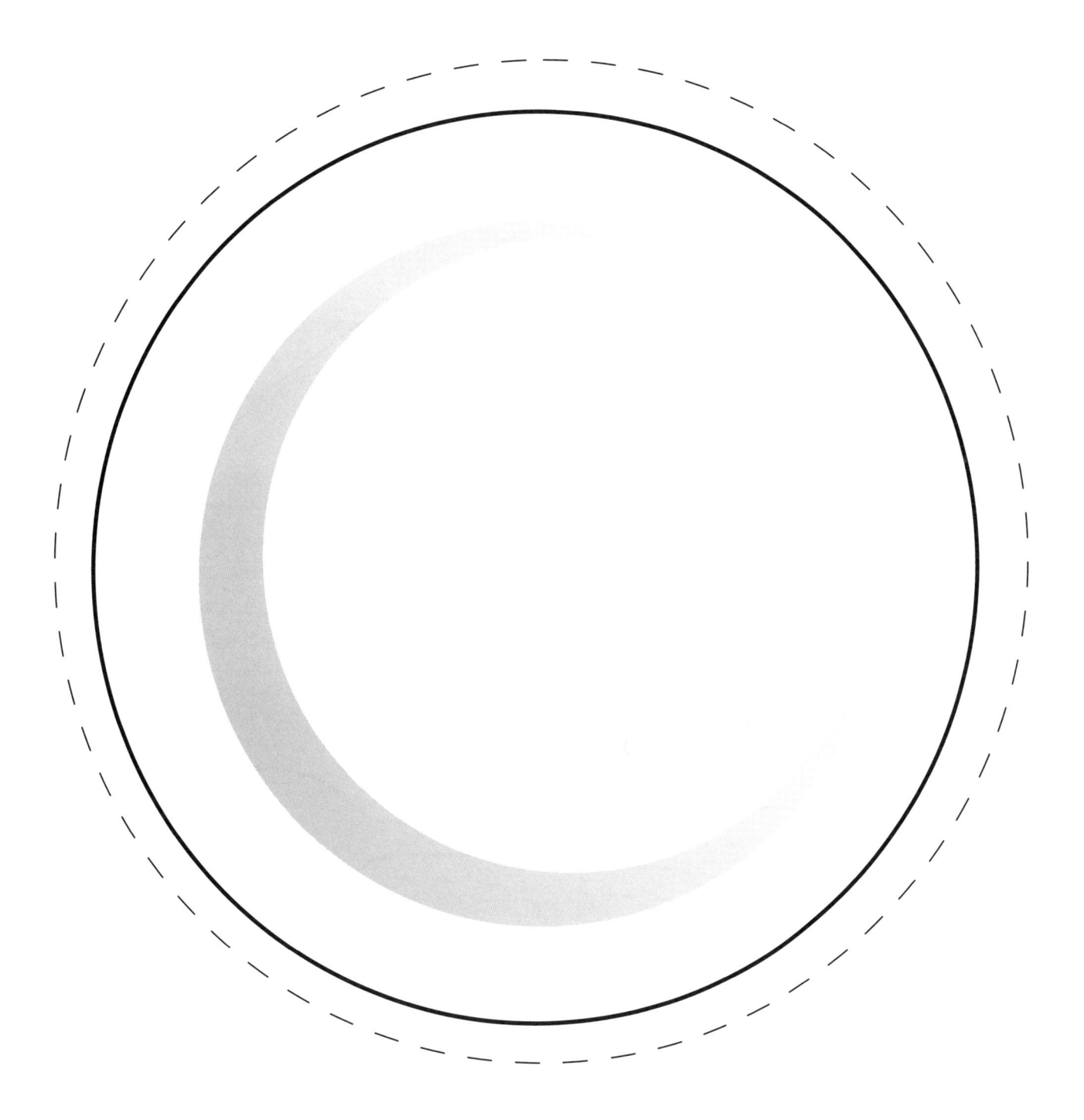

Concepts, cont.

Unit 1
Blooming Category Activities   17   Copyright © 2006 LinguiSystems, Inc.

Food

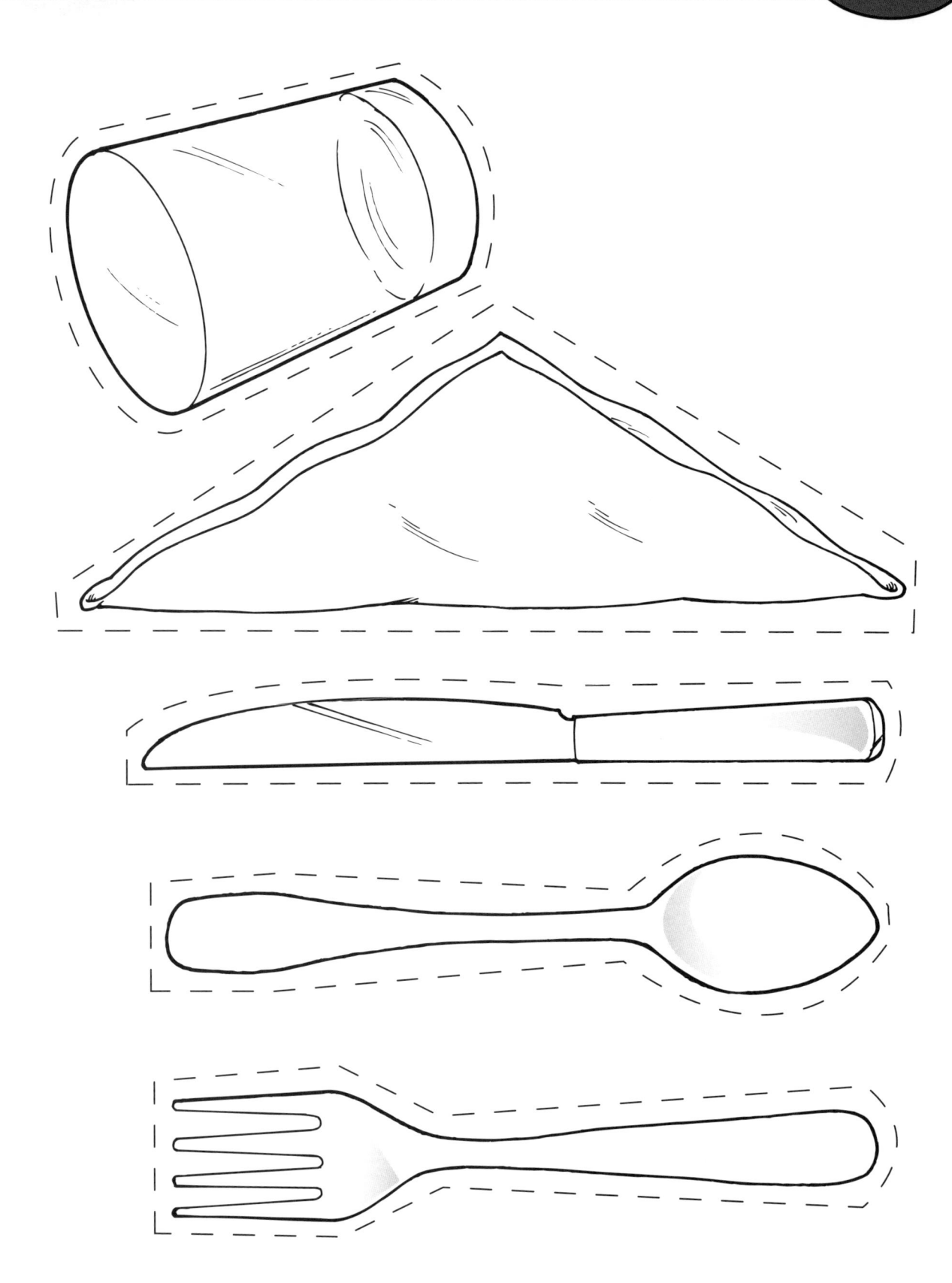

Concepts, cont.

Unit 1
Blooming Category Activities

Food

Bloom's Taxonomy

→ **Objective:** The child will answer increasingly more difficult questions about food based on *Bloom's Taxonomy of Educational Objectives*.

Ask these questions while doing the Paper Plate Meals activity on page 9 and throughout all the activities in this lesson.

Knowledge
- What food did you put on both plates?
- How many fruits did we use?
- Name all the lunch foods.
- Who cooks dinner at your house?

Comprehension
- Tell how we made our plates.
- Describe one food on the dinner plate.
- Choose a breakfast food. Tell how it tastes.
- What does *meal* mean?

Application
- What else could we have for lunch?
- Have you ever helped cook at home? Tell about it.
- It's time for breakfast and there is no cereal in the house. What do you do?
- Think of another word for *beverage*.

Analysis
- How are popcorn and pretzels the same?
- Look at the breakfast and dinner plates. How are they different?
- During the day, which meal comes first? In the middle? Last?
- What is the opposite of *empty*?

Synthesis
- Create your own dinner menu.
- We put food on our paper plates. Where else can you put food?
- Suppose you have pancakes and no syrup. What would you do?
- What would it be like if Mom did not know how to cook?

Evaluation
- Which is your favorite meal? Why?
- Is it okay to eat breakfast food at dinner? Why?
- What food do you like best? What food do you like least?

Animals

Project

Fishing

Materials:
- picture cards on pages 21-23
- stick for fishing pole
- string
- magnet
- metal paper clips
- barn, house, and zoo – These could be toys; small, decorated cardboard boxes; or pictures.

Directions:
- Make a fishing pole by tying some string to the end of a stick and then tying a magnet onto the end of the string.
- Put a paper clip on each animal picture card and scatter the picture cards facedown on the table or floor.
- Take turns "fishing" for a picture card. After catching a "fish," name the animal, and then place it in its proper habitat.
- When you have finished the activity, name some other animals that could go in each group.

Animals

Picture Cards

➡ **Objective**: The child will increase receptive understanding and expressive use of vocabulary related to animals.

bear	bird	cat
chicken	cow	dog
duck	elephant	fish

Unit 2
Blooming Category Activities

Copyright © 2006 LinguiSystems, Inc.

Animals

Picture Cards, cont.

giraffe	goat	horse
kangaroo	lion	monkey
owl	penguin	pig

Unit 2
Blooming Category Activities

Animals

Picture Cards, cont.

rabbit	rooster	seal
sheep	tiger	turkey
turtle	whale	zebra

Unit 2
Blooming Category Activities

Animals

Family Letter

Dear Family,

In speech, we are learning about animals and the vocabulary that goes with this category. Please help your child use this vocabulary at home. Talk about the picture below with your child and help him use the target words. Then put this page up somewhere in your home to remind everyone to help your child talk about animals. This would be a great time to take a trip to the zoo or to check out some animal books from your school or local library. Some ideas to encourage use of animal vocabulary are included at the bottom of this page.

Thank you, _____

Name all of the animals you see in this pet store.
Which one would you like to have? Why? What would you name your pet?

- Let's feed the **ducks** some bread.
- The **blue jay** is on a **birdbath**.
- Please take the **dog** for a walk.
- We saw a **giraffe** at the **zoo**.
- Our **cat** had baby **kittens**.

- I can swim like a **fish**.
- Let's hop like a **bunny**.
- I love to ride **horses**.
- There's a **frog** on the sidewalk.
- Let's read a book about **lions** and **tigers**.

Unit 2
Blooming Category Activities

Animals

Activities

For some of these activities, you will photocopy and cut apart the picture cards on pages 21-23.

- Sort the picture cards into the following groups: *farm, zoo, pets, water animals*, and a*nimals with feathers*. (Some of the pictures could go in more than one category.)

- While playing with a stuffed animal or a puppet, have the child use size, shape, color, and texture adjectives to describe the toy.

- Let a child pull a picture card out of a toy barn and then make the sound that the animal on the card makes. Have the other children guess the animal.

- Let the child think of an animal and demonstrate how that animal moves. Have the other children guess the animal and use verbs to describe the action.

- While playing with a toy barn and animals, encourage the child to use prepositional phrases, such as *in the barn, beside the gate*, and *next to the cow*.

- Tape some of the zoo animal pictures on the wall around the room. Let the children "visit the zoo." Have them name and describe the animals they see as they walk around the room.

- Give a child two of the animal picture cards or two toy animals and ask him to tell two ways the animals are the same and two ways they are different.

- Sing "Old MacDonald Had a Farm" and let the children take turns naming what animal and sound to sing for each verse.

- Have the child draw a picture of or bring in a photo of his pet or an animal he has seen. Then have him tell about the animal.

- Take a poll within the group or around the school. Ask, "Which of these pets is your favorite: a dog, a cat, or a bird?" Encourage the use of words such as *some, more, most, few, more than,* and *less than* when discussing the poll results.

- Glue the picture cards onto index cards or construction paper to make a booklet of zoo animals. Then take a field trip to the zoo or look in a zoo book. Have the children name, discuss, and check off the animals that they see.

- Choose some of the picture cards and talk about what kinds of food those animals eat.

- Have Goldfish crackers or animal cookies for a snack. Let the children name, count, and describe the treats.

- Choose the appropriate picture cards to talk about the names of baby animals, such as *kittens, lambs, puppies*, and *bunnies*.

- Let the children take turns as line leader. Have the line leader tell the other children to do things such as *hop like a bunny, fly like a bird, crawl like a turtle, waddle like a duck*, or *gallop like a horse*.

- Use Play-Doh and small sticks to make a bird nest and eggs to put in the nest. Talk about the sequence of events from a bird building a nest to new birds flying away.

Animals

Worksheet

Objective: The child will increase receptive understanding and expressive use of vocabulary related to animals while sequencing pictures and describing those sequences.

Directions:
- Photocopy and cut out the sequence pictures on page 27.
- Let the children put the pictures in three story groups.
- Have the children glue the pictures in the correct sequences onto the boxes below.
- Then let the children take turns telling about their sequence stories.

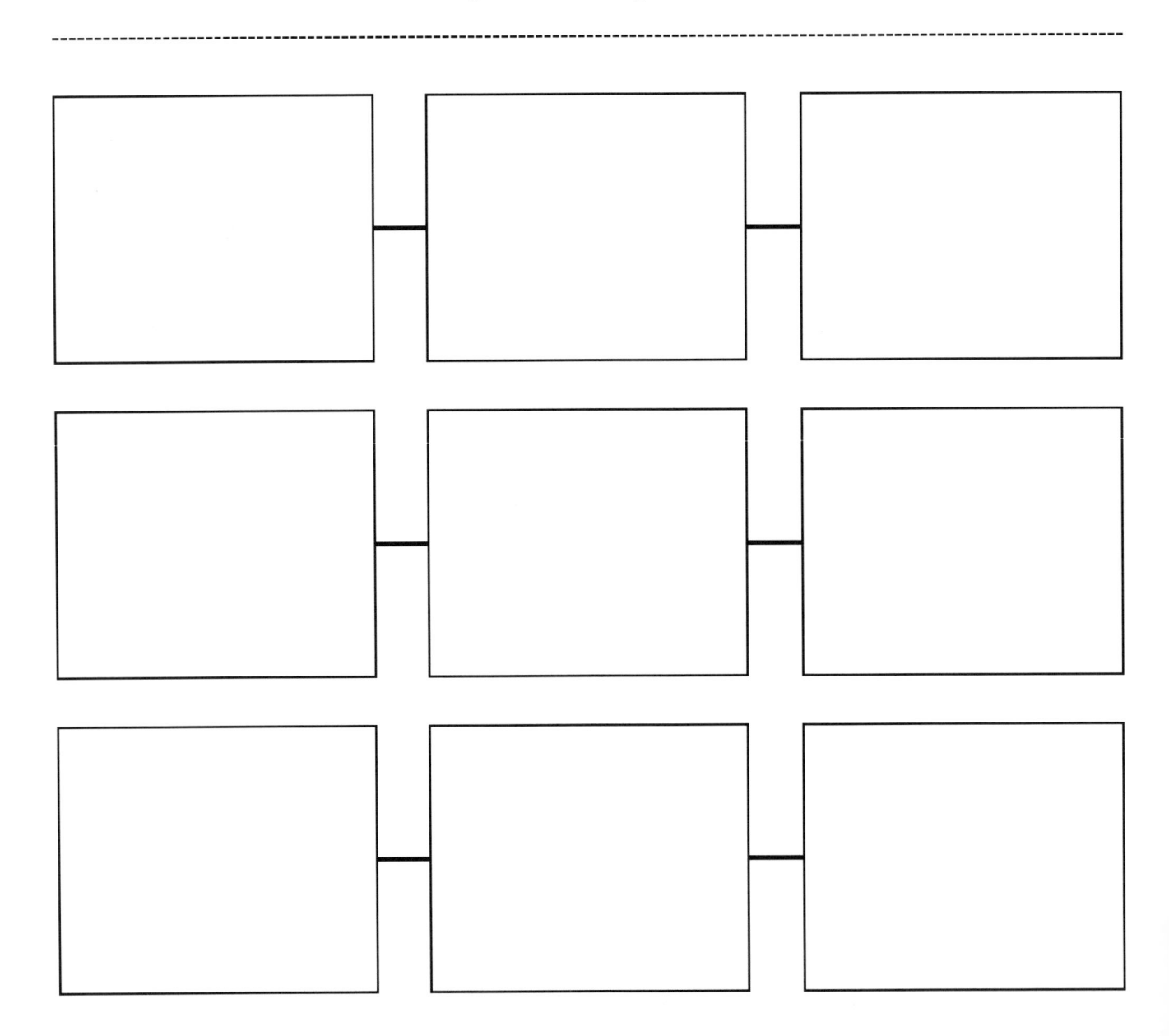

Unit 2
Blooming Category Activities

Copyright © 2006 LinguiSystems, Inc.

Animals

Worksheet, *cont.*

Unit 2
Blooming Category Activities

Animals

Concepts

➡️ **Objective**: The child will demonstrate receptive understanding and expressive use of basic concepts while completing the activity.

Animals and Their Homes

Materials:
- photocopies of pages 29 and 30 for each child
- scissors
- glue
- crayons or markers

Directions:
- Be sure that the children can name the animals and the animal homes.
- Cut out or let the children cut out the animals on page 29.
- If desired, let the children color the pictures.
- Have the children follow your spatial directions as they glue the animals in and around the animal homes on page 30.

Suggested Concepts to Target:

- **over/under**
  Put the bird **over** the nest.
  Draw a line **under** the nest.

- **left/right**
  Glue the dog to the **left** of the doghouse.
  Put an X on the **right** side of the doghouse.

- **center/row**
  Put the fish in the **center** of the fishbowl.
  Draw a **row** of fish in the fishbowl.

- **in/out**
  Draw the baby kangaroo **in** its mother's pouch.
  Glue the bear coming **out** of the cave.

- **on/off**
  Glue the frog **on** a lily pad.
  Make an X **off** of the lily pad.

- **top/middle/bottom**
  Draw a nest in the **top** of the tree.
  Color a branch in the **middle** of the tree.
  Draw a box at the **bottom** of the tree.

- **before/after**
  What did you glue on **before** you glued the frog?
  After you cut out the bear, color it.

Animals

Concepts, cont.

Unit 2
Blooming Category Activities

Concepts, cont.

Animals

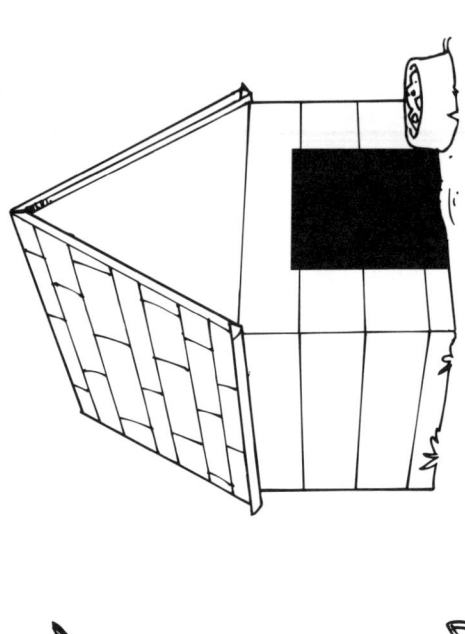

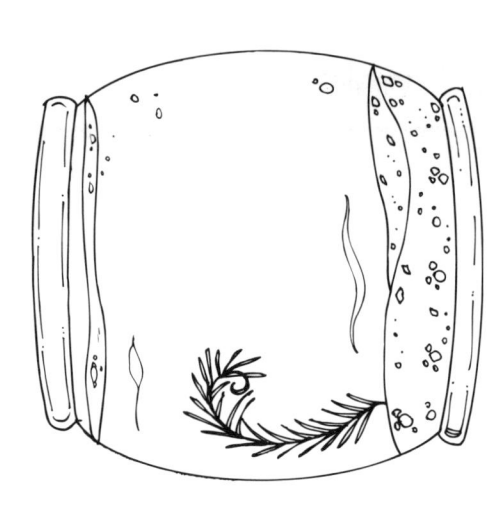

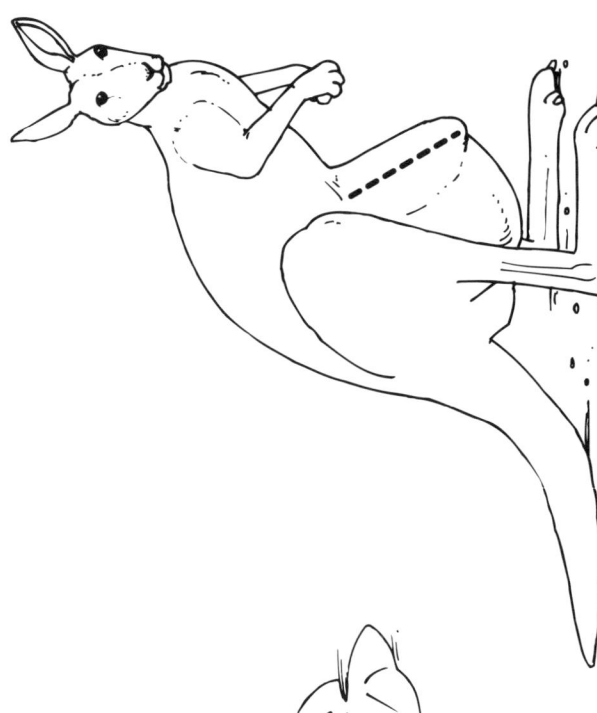

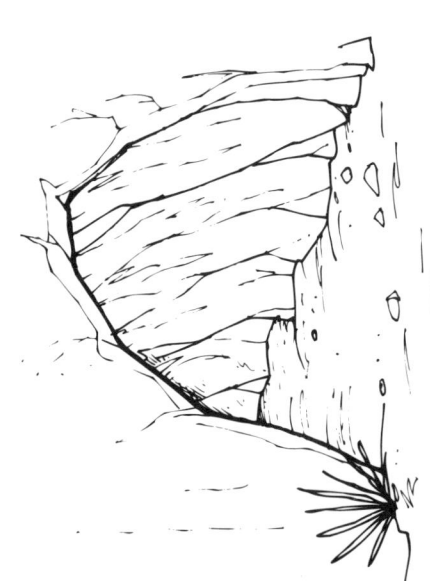

Unit 2
Blooming Category Activities 30 Copyright © 2006 LinguiSystems, Inc.

Animals

Bloom's Taxonomy

➤ **Objective**: The child will answer increasingly more difficult questions about animals based on *Bloom's Taxonomy of Educational Objectives*.

Ask these questions while doing the Fishing activity on page 20 and throughout all of the activities in this lesson.

Knowledge
- How many fish did you catch?
- What animals did you put in the zoo?
- Where did you put the cow?
- What sound does a cat make?

Comprehension
- How did we catch the fish?
- Give a definition for the word *pet*.
- Describe what a giraffe looks like.
- Tell me two animals that are fast.

Application
- Have you ever been fishing? Tell about it.
- Name three animals that live in the water and three that fly in the sky.
- What would be wrong with having an elephant for a pet?
- What group of animals contains a duck, a turkey, and a chicken?

Analysis
- Tell two ways that a horse is different from a zebra.
- How are a duck and a turkey alike?
- A zebra has stripes. A leopard has _____.
- What animal did we catch first? Which one did we catch last?

Synthesis
- What is another way that we could pretend to catch fish?
- Create a new kind of animal and tell about it.
- Draw a picture of an animal you would like to be.
- What would it be like if animals could speak our language?

Evaluation
- What is your favorite kind of pet? Why?
- Would you rather visit a zoo or a farm? Why?
- Rate these animals from best to worst for riding: camel, horse, and donkey. Tell about your decision.

Body Parts

Project

Tracing Body Outlines

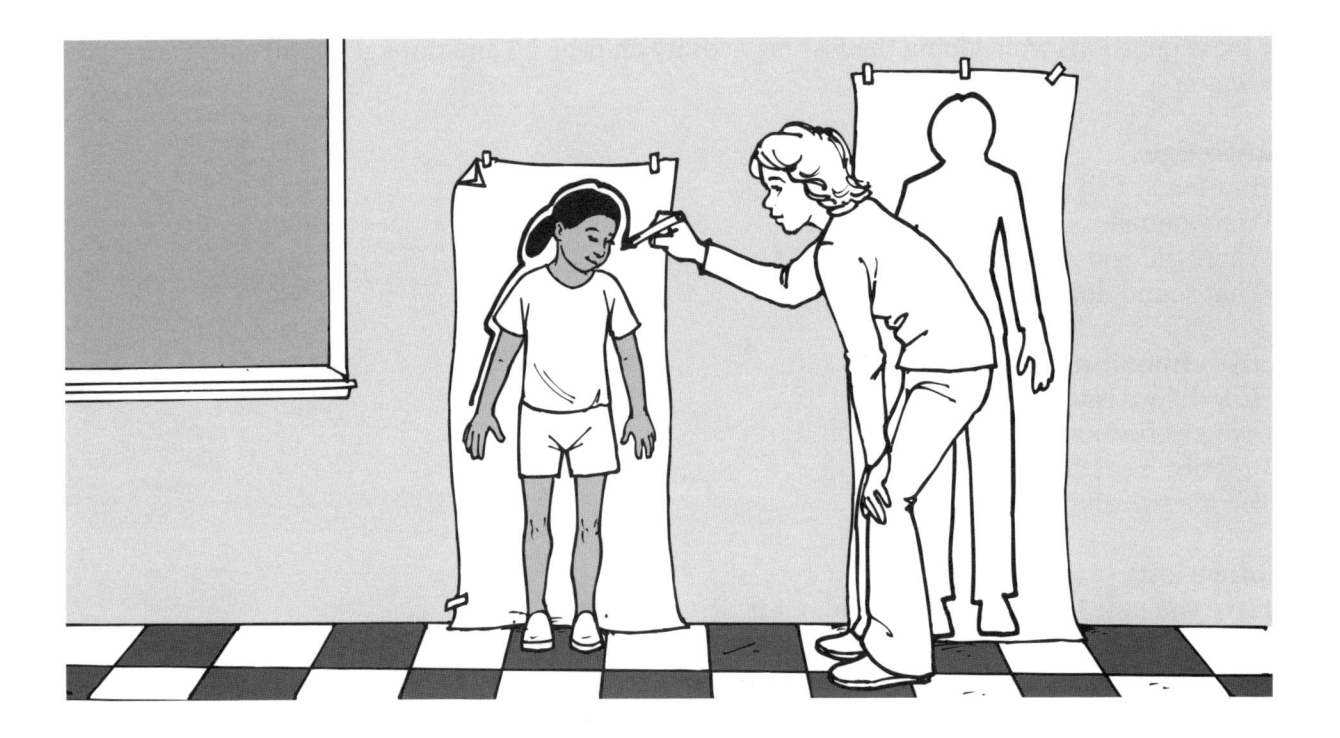

Materials:
- a roll of craft or butcher paper
- scissors
- tape
- crayons

Directions:
- Cut lengths of paper tall enough for the teacher and each child.
- Tape the paper vertically on the wall.
- Before the session, get someone to trace an outline of the teacher's body.
- Have one child stand with her back against one of the sheets of paper.
- Use a crayon to trace an outline of the child's body.
- Name and discuss the body parts as they are being traced.

Body Parts

Picture Cards

⇨ **Objective**: The child will increase receptive understanding and expressive use of body parts vocabulary.

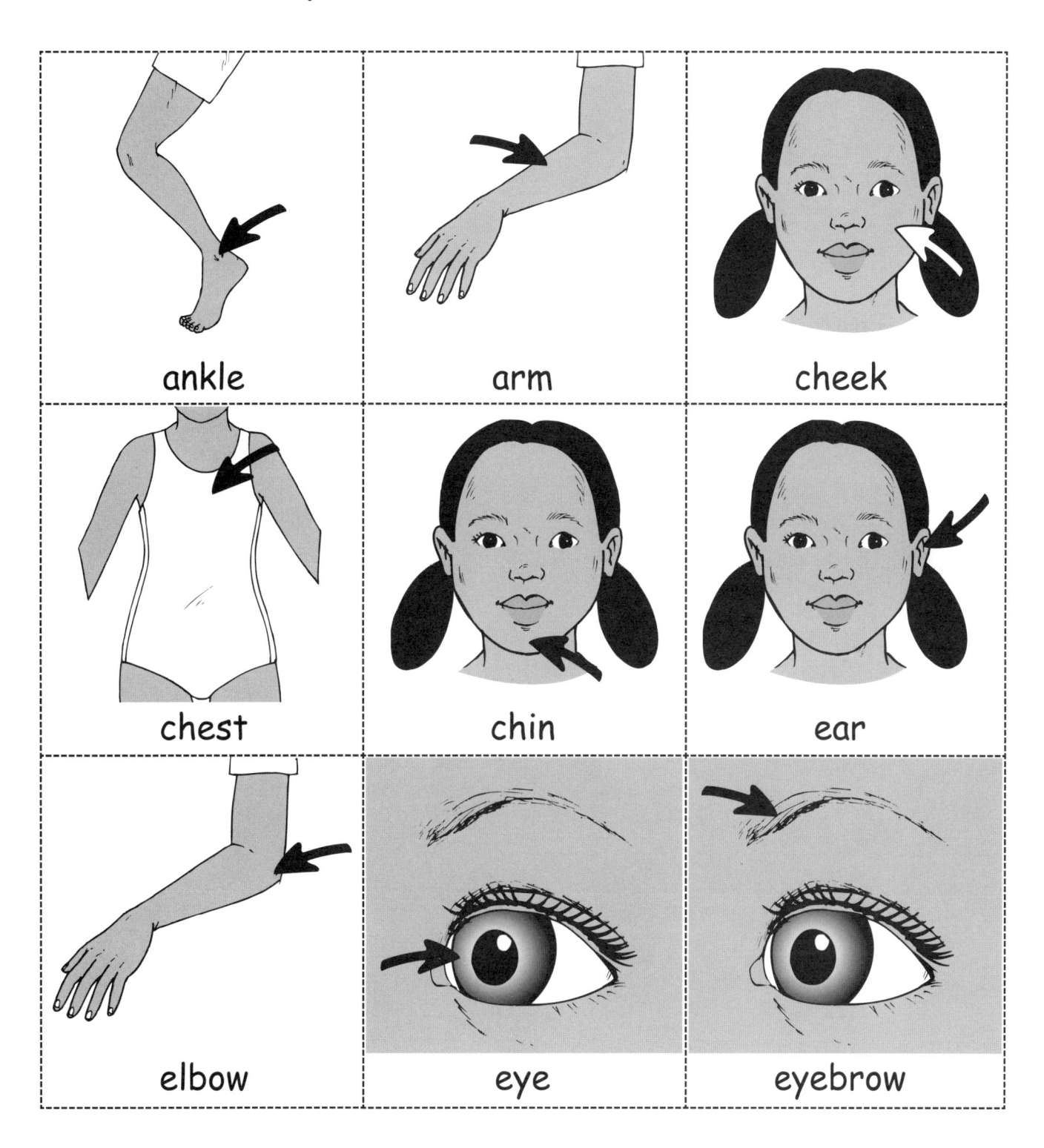

ankle	arm	cheek
chest	chin	ear
elbow	eye	eyebrow

Unit 3
Blooming Category Activities

Body Parts

Picture Cards, cont.

finger	foot	forehead
hand	knee	leg
lip	neck	nose

Unit 3
Blooming Category Activities

34

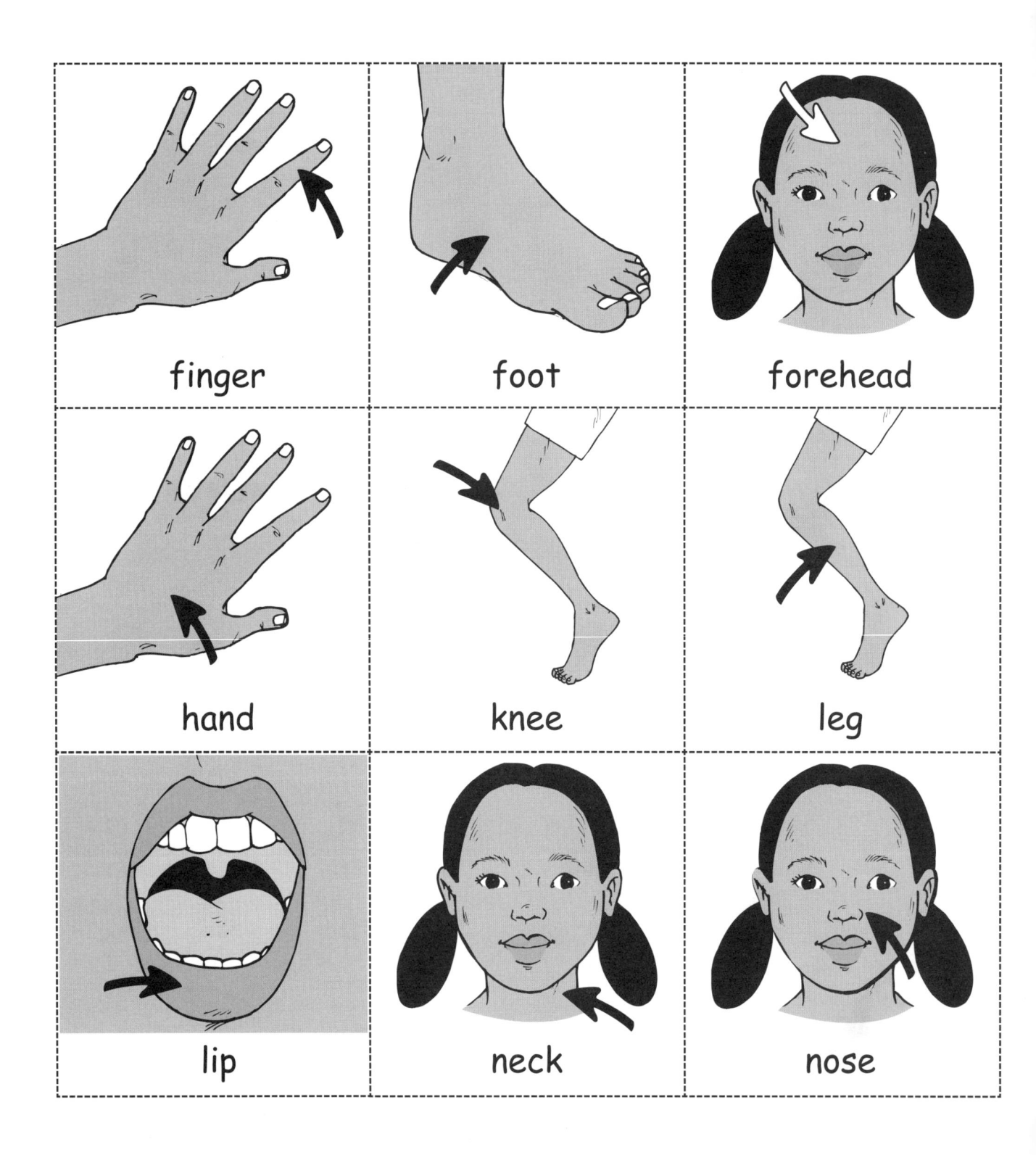

Copyright © 2006 LinguiSystems, Inc.

Body Parts

Picture Cards, cont.

shoulder	stomach	tooth
thigh	thumb	toe
tongue	waist	wrist

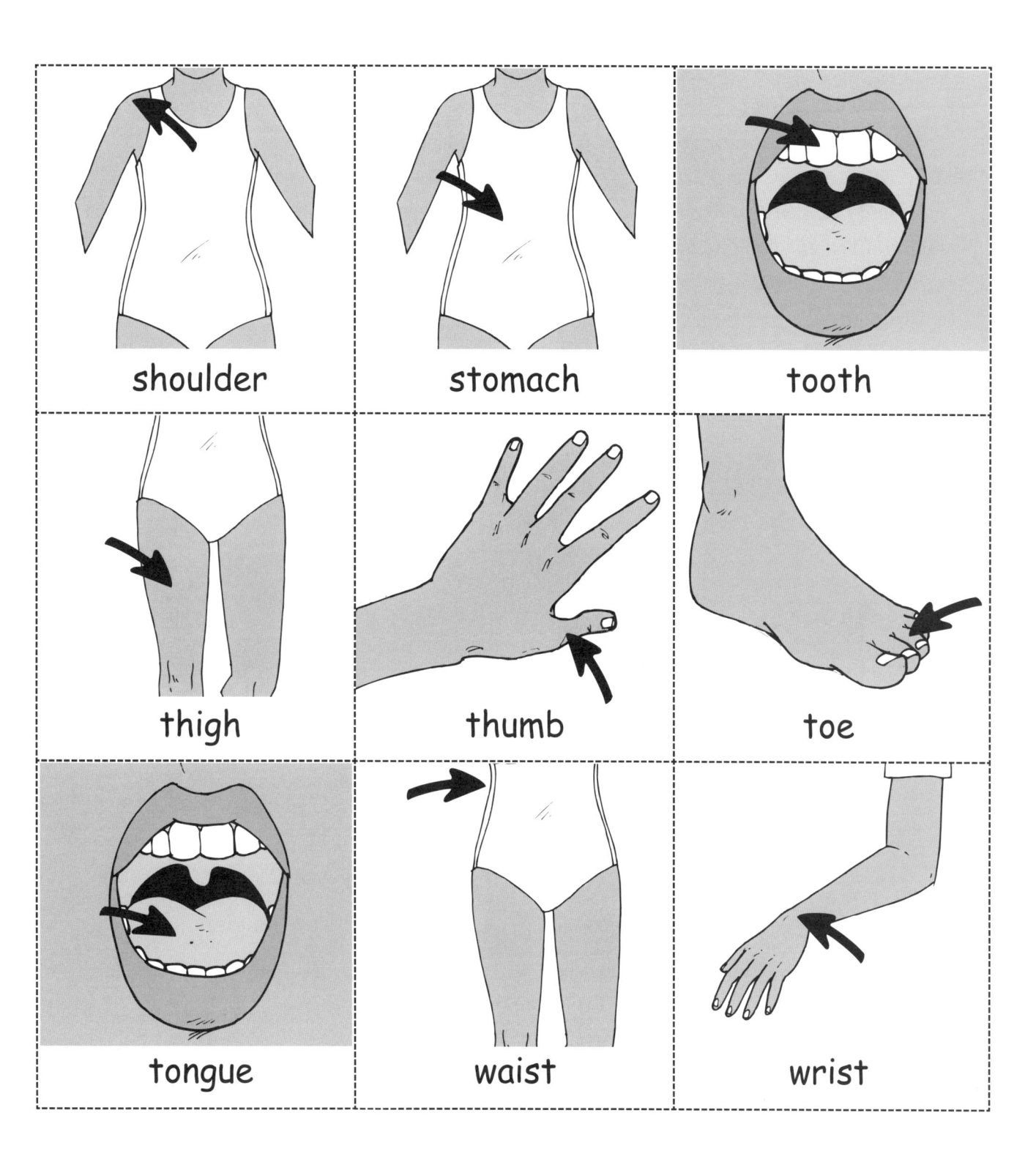

Unit 3
Blooming Category Activities

Body Parts

Family Letter

Dear Family,

In speech, we are learning about body parts and the vocabulary that goes with this category. You can help your child practice this vocabulary at home. Talk about the picture with your child and help her use the target words. Then put this page on your refrigerator or in another high traffic area to remind everyone to help your child talk about body parts. Some ideas to encourage this practice are listed at the bottom of the page.

Thank you, _____

What body parts are these children using at the playground?
Name three of your body parts and tell how they help you play.

- I have five **toes** on each **foot**.
- Your belt goes around your **waist**.
- Pull your socks up over your **ankles**.
- My hat goes on my **head**.
- Let's sing "**Head**, **Shoulders**, **Knees**, and **Toes**."

- Mom's **eyes** are blue.
- My doll has two **hands**.
- Our puppy has four **legs**.
- Dad's tie goes around his **neck**.
- Wear the bracelet on your **wrist**.

Unit 3
Blooming Category Activities

Body Parts

Activities

For some of these activities, you will photocopy and cut apart the picture cards on pages 33-35.

- Hang a traced body outline on the wall. Have the child pull a picture card from a bag, name the body part, and then tape it to the corresponding body part of the outline.

- After the child names and points to all of the body parts in the song, sing "Head, Shoulders, Knees, and Toes."

- Have the child name body parts as she washes a doll in a toy bathtub.

- Have the child name body parts as she dresses a doll.

- Play dress-up. As the child puts on each piece of clothing, have her say where she wears it. For instance, she might say, "I put a scarf around my neck" or "This ring goes on my finger."

- Play "Simon Says." Use body part instructions such as *Put your elbow on your knee* or *Touch your eyebrow with your thumb*.

- Have the child categorize the picture cards into bags that say "face" and "body," or "above the waist" and "below the waist."

- Let each child pull a picture card out of a bag, name it, and tell what she uses it for. For instance, she might say, "I use my legs to walk."

- Make several copies of the picture card pages. Cut out the pictures, glue them onto cards, and play "Body-Part Bingo."

- Put the picture cards in a stack and have the child choose a card. Ask her to name the body part and put a sticker on the corresponding body part of a doll or a body outline.

- Discuss the five senses. Have the child relate her eyes, ears, nose, hands, and mouth to objects such as *paintings, bells, perfume, cotton balls,* and *pieces of candy*. For example, she might say, "I use my ears to hear the bell ring" or "I use my nose to smell perfume."

- Compare eye color and the size of arms, legs, feet, hands, fingers, and toes between two children or between a child and the teacher.

- Pull pieces of clothing and accessories out of a suitcase and have the child tell where on her body she would wear each one.

- Using a toy doll and a pretend doctor's kit, let the child talk about body parts as she puts on bandages, takes the doll's temperature, gives injections, listens for a heartbeat, etc.

- As you sing and play the "Hokey Pokey," let the children take turns deciding what body part to "put in and out."

Body Parts

Worksheet

Objective: The child will match body parts with associated objects and will use verbs to describe the association.

Say, "Name the body parts on the left side of the page. Now draw a line to the picture on the right side of the page that goes with each body part. Tell about it in a sentence." The child could say, "You stand on a skateboard with your feet."

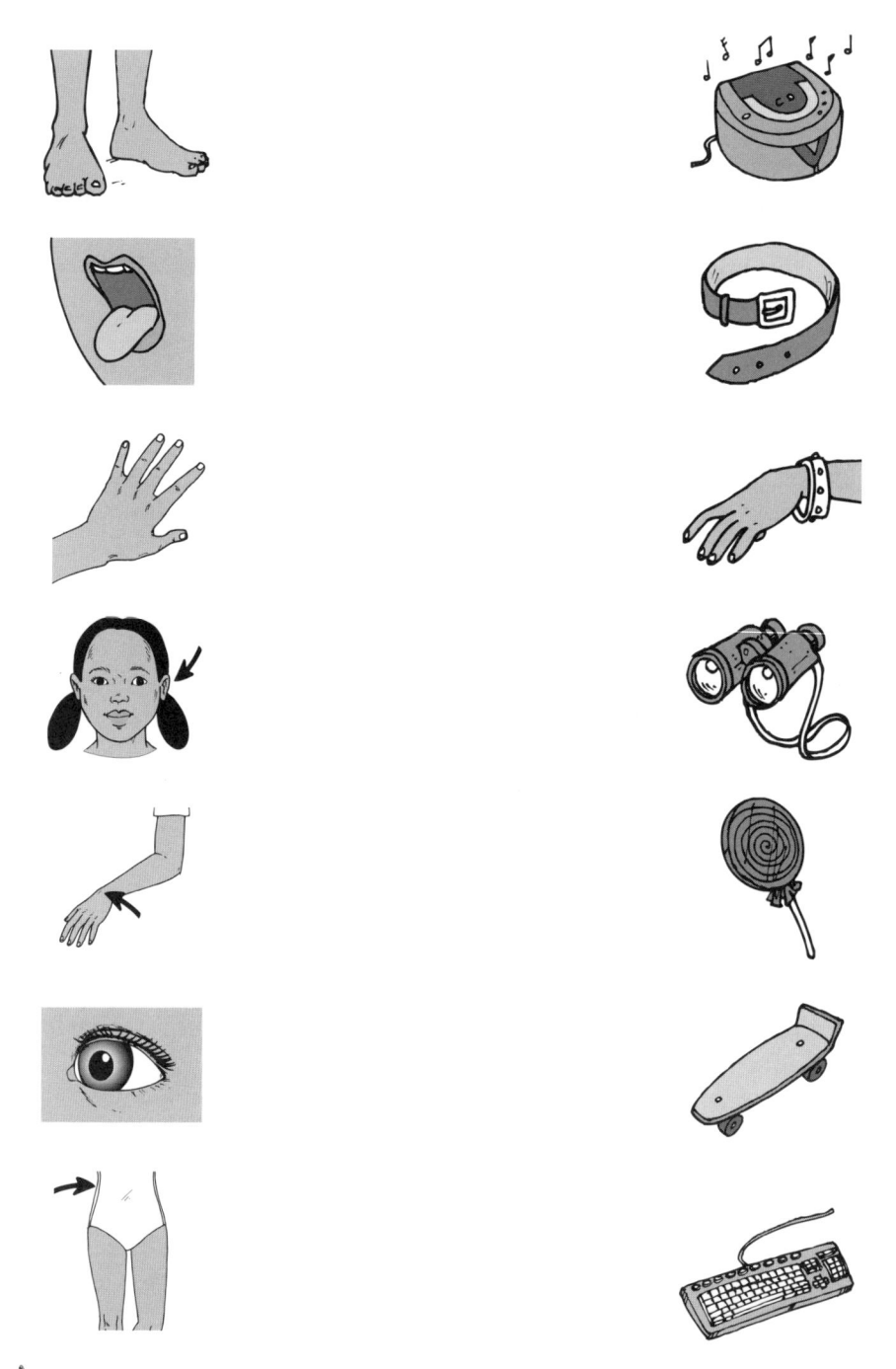

Unit 3
Blooming Category Activities 38 Copyright © 2006 LinguiSystems, Inc.

Body Parts

Concepts

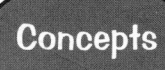

➡️ **Objective**: The child will demonstrate receptive understanding and expressive use of basic concepts while completing the activity.

Paper Plate Face

Materials:
- photocopies of pages 40 and 41 for each child
- paper plates
- crayons or markers
- glue
- scissors

Directions: See page 40.

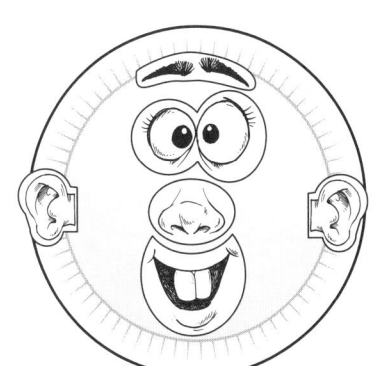

Suggested Concepts to Target:

- **top/middle/bottom**
  The eyebrows are towards the **top** of the face.
  The nose is in the **middle** of the face.
  The mouth is at the **bottom** of the face.

- **side**
  The ears are on the **side** of the face.

- **above/below**
  The eyebrows are **above** the eyes.
  The mouth is **below** the nose.

- **same/different**
  How are the face you made and the face your friend made the **same**?
  How are they **different**?

- **first/middle/last**
  What is the **first** thing you did to make your face plate?
  What did you glue in the **middle** of the plate?
  What did you do **last**?

- **left/right**
  What did you put on the **left** side of the plate?
  Show me the **right** side of your plate.

- **all/some/none**
  Did you use **all**, **some**, or **none** of the face parts?

- **whole/half**
  Show me the **whole** face you made.
  Show me **half** of the face you made.

Body Parts

Concepts, cont.

Directions: Say, "Look at the parts of a face on this page and on page 41. Choose a mouth, a nose, a pair of eyes, a pair of ears, and a pair of eyebrows. Color them. Then cut them out and glue them on your plate to make a funny face."

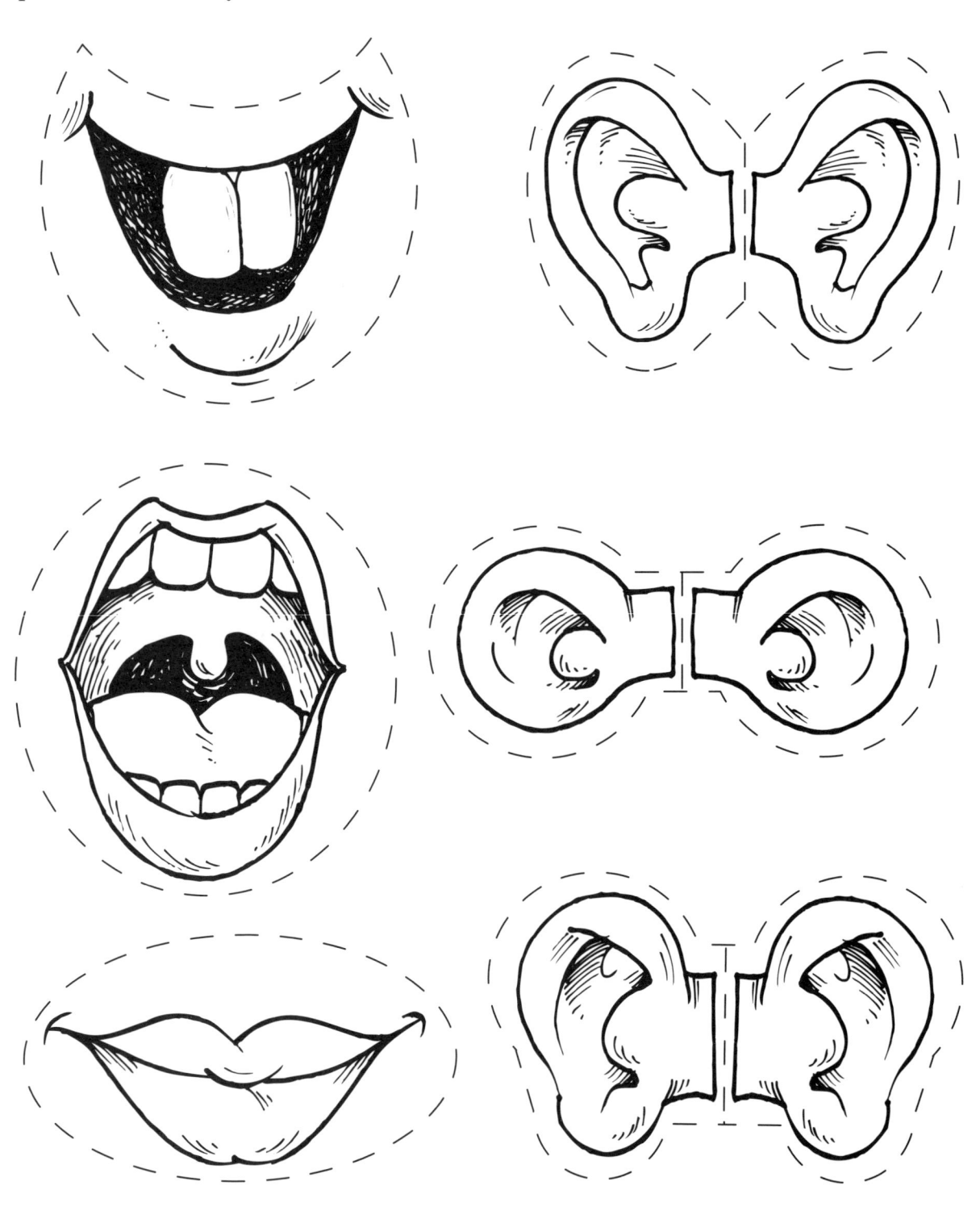

Unit 3
Blooming Category Activities

Body Parts

Concepts, cont.

Unit 3
Blooming Category Activities

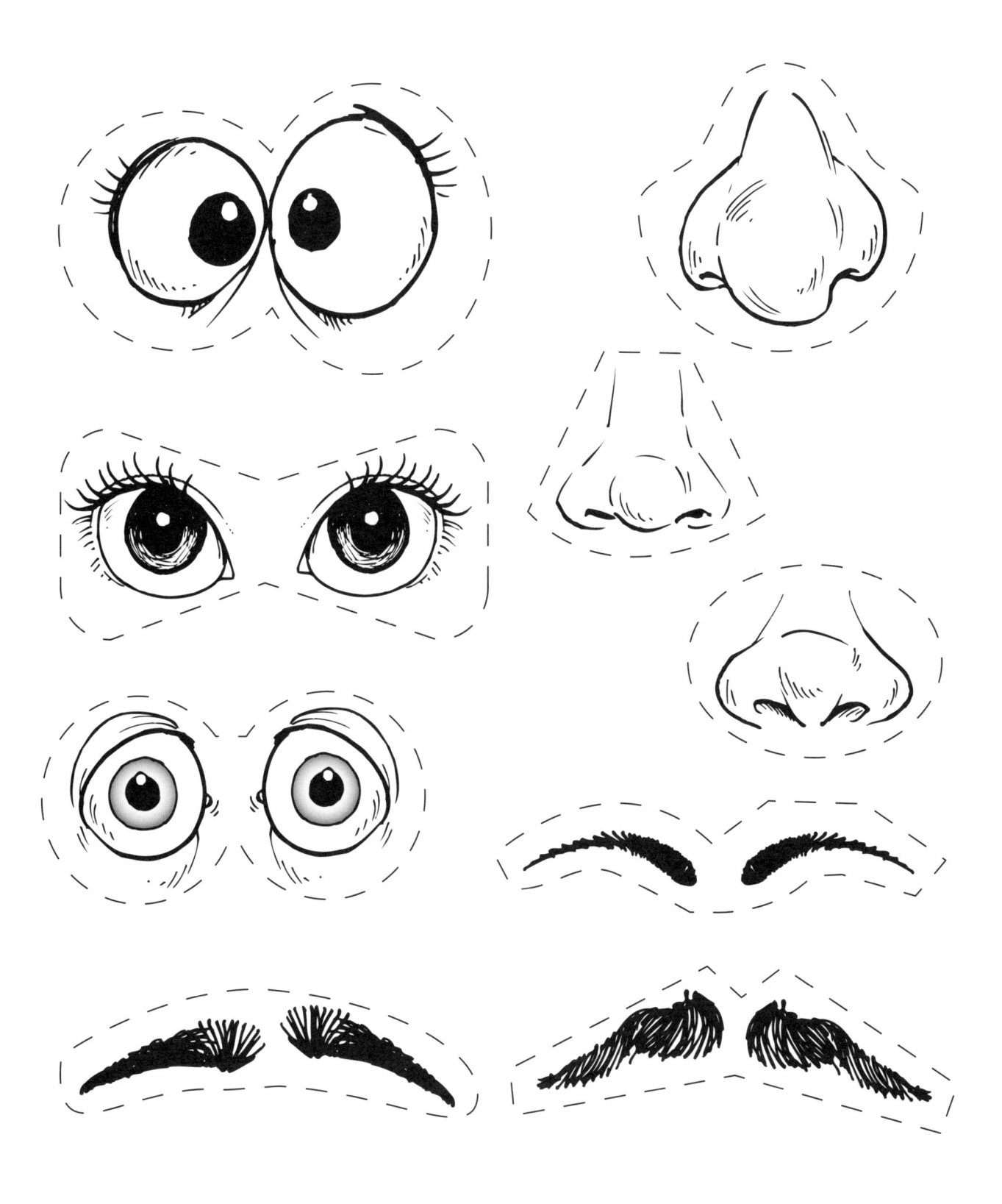

Body Parts

Bloom's Taxonomy

Objective: The child will answer increasingly more difficult questions about body parts based on *Bloom's Taxonomy of Educational Objectives*.

Ask these questions while doing the Tracing Body Outlines activity on page 32 and throughout all of the activities in this lesson.

Knowledge
- How many body parts are on your face?
- What body part is in the middle of your face?
- Where is your elbow?
- Look at the outline of your body and name eight parts.

Comprehension
- How did we trace your body?
- Describe the outline of your body.
- Explain how your knees help you walk.
- What does the word *trace* mean?

Application
- Show me your knuckle.
- Did you ever break a bone in your body? Tell about it.
- What if we couldn't tape the paper on the wall? How could we trace our bodies?
- People have legs. What else has legs?

Analysis
- Look at our two outlines. How are they the same? How are they different?
- What was the first thing we did to trace our bodies? What was the last thing?
- How is a person's body like a dog's body? How is it different?
- Why do we need elbows and knees?

Synthesis
- Think of all the things you can do with your feet.
- What would it be like if our hands were on our legs?
- Pretend that you had to build a model of a body. What could you use?
- What do you think it would be like if we had three eyes?

Evaluation
- Some people are tall and some people are short. Do you think it is better to be tall or short? Why?
- What part of your leg is the most important? Why?
- Which body part is more important to you—your ears to hear or your eyes to see? Why?

Clothing

Project

Dressing a Doll

Materials:
- doll
- doll clothes that can be for different seasons or temperatures (Clothing might include a shirt, pants, shorts, tennis shoes, slippers, pajamas, a coat, a hat, gloves, and a swimsuit.)

Directions:
- The child selects a piece of clothing and names it.
- He tells when you would wear it and then puts it on the doll.
- Also discuss the names of the various parts of the item, such as *the shirt has a sleeve, a collar, a cuff, and buttons.*

Clothing

Picture Cards

Objective: The child will increase receptive understanding and expressive use of clothing vocabulary.

belt	boots	coat
collar	cuff	dress
gloves	hat	mittens

Unit 4
Blooming Category Activities

44

Copyright © 2006 LinguiSystems, Inc.

Clothing

Picture Cards, *cont.*

pajamas	pants	robe
sandals	scarf	shirt
shorts	skirt	sleeve

Unit 4
Blooming Category Activities

Clothing

Picture Cards, cont.

slippers	socks	suit
sweater	swimsuit	tennis shoes
tie	underwear	zipper

Unit 4
Blooming Category Activities

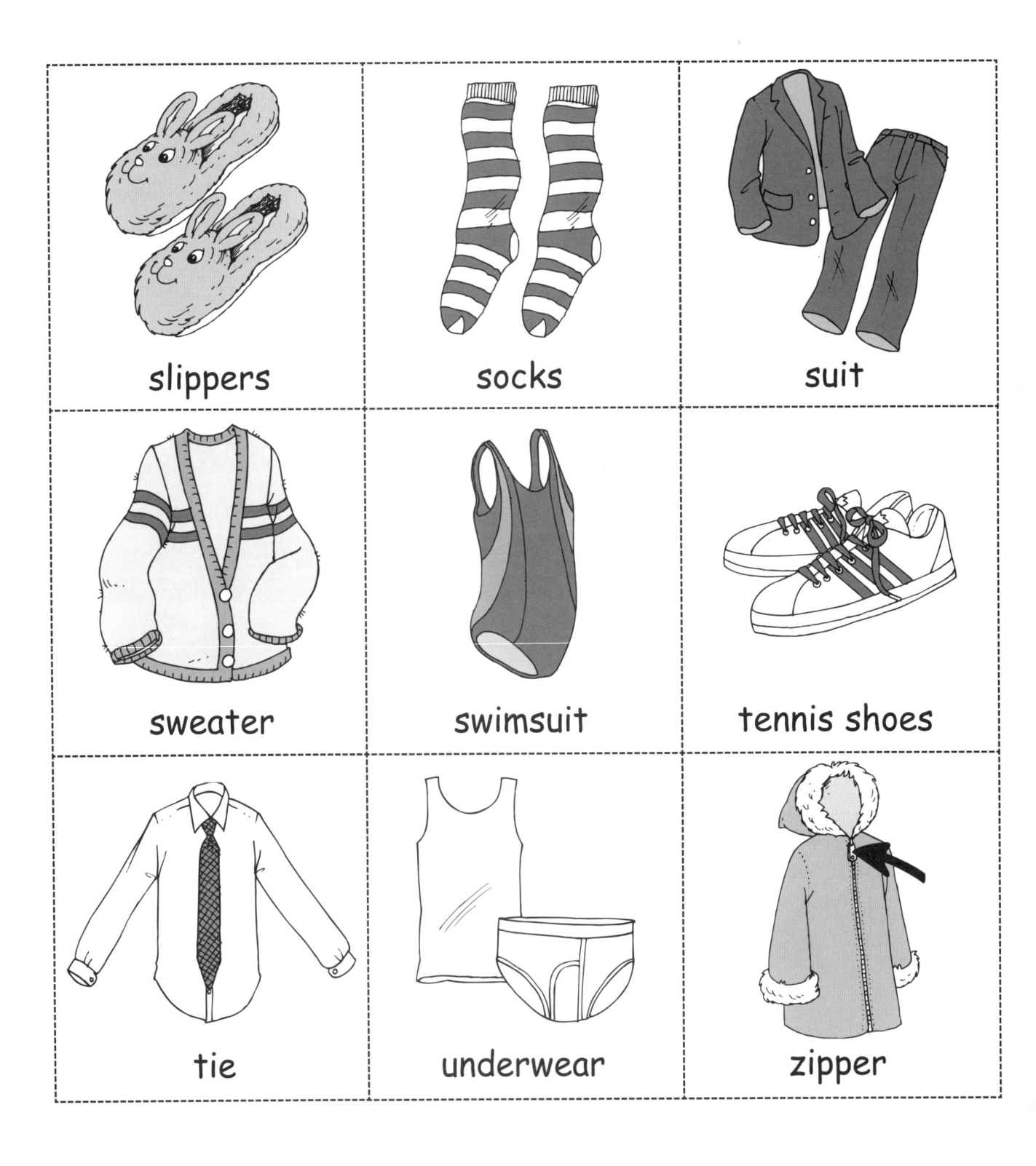

Clothing

Family Letter

Dear Family,

In speech, we are learning about clothing and the vocabulary that goes with that category. You can help your child practice this vocabulary at home. Talk about the picture below with your child and help him use clothing words to answer the questions. Then put this page in a high traffic area in your home to remind everyone to help your child talk about clothing. Some ideas to encourage this are listed at the bottom of the page.

Thank you, _____

What are you going to wear to school today?
Name the clothes you see in the closet. Is there something you could wear to school?

- Your **pants** need a **belt**.
- Wear your **sandals** to the beach.
- We got Dad a **tie**.
- That **shoe** goes on your left foot.
- Don't forget your baseball **cap**.

- My **shirt** has a stain on it.
- Put your dirty **clothes** in the **laundry**.
- Hang your **coat** on the hook.
- Mom wore a **dress** to the party.
- These **pants** have lots of **pockets**.

Unit 4
Blooming Category Activities

Clothing

Activities

For some of these activities, you will photocopy and cut apart the picture cards on pages 44-46.

- Have the child choose a picture card and name it. Then have him tell what body part the clothing goes on.

- Have the child choose a picture card and name it. Then have him decide if he would wear it in hot or cold weather.

- Put doll clothes in a bag and have the child pull out one clothing item. Then let him name the item and tell if it is something a boy, a girl, or both would wear.

- Let the child choose a picture card, name it, and then pack it in a toy suitcase.

- Let the child compare his shoes to the teacher's and talk about how they are the same and how they are different.

- Have the child grab a clothing picture card from a bag. Let him name the item and then pretend to put it on.

- Gather some old clothes. Then let the child play dress-up while he talks about the clothes, using sentences containing prepositional phrases, such as *The belt goes around my waist*, *I put a hat on my head*, and *The tie goes around my neck*.

- Put various clothing items around the room, and have the child go shopping for the clothes. Each time he "buys" an item, have him tell when he would wear it.

- Describe real clothing items using color, size, and texture adjectives.

- Gather socks of various sizes and colors. Have the child sort them by size and by color.

- Sing "This Is the Way" and use verbs that are associated with clothing, such as *zip*, *button*, *tie*, *put on*, and *snap*.

Clothing

Worksheet

Objective: The child will increase his understanding and use of clothing vocabulary and associated parts.

Materials:
- one copy of the picture on page 50 for each child
- crayons or markers

Directions:
- Have the child look at the picture of the pants and shirt.
- Ask him to listen to and follow your directions.

   * Put a line under a pants pocket.

   * Draw an X on the shirt collar.

   * Color one shirt sleeve blue.

   * Circle one leg of the pants.

   * Color the zipper black.

   * Draw a line on a seam in the pants.

   * Put a box around one of the belt loops.

   * Color the shirt buttons red.

Clothing

Worksheet, *cont.*

Clothing

Concepts

→ **Objective**: The child will demonstrate receptive understanding and expressive use of basic concepts while completing the activity.

On the Clothesline

Materials:
- clothesline made from string or yarn
- a photocopy of the clothing pictures on page 52 for each child
- paper clips or clothespins

Directions:
- String the clothesline across the board or between two chairs.
- Have the child cut out the clothing pictures and place them facedown on a table.
- Let the child pick a picture and name the clothing item.
- Use concepts to tell the child where to paper clip the picture, such as *Hang the* **large** *shirt* **next to** *the* **small** *shoe, Hang the tennis shoes on the* **right** *side of the slippers*, and *Hang the* **large** *button* **beside** *the* **small** *button*.

Suggested Concepts to Target:

• **next to/beside**	Put the large shirt **next to** the small button. The slippers are **beside** the long socks.
• **first/middle/last**	I put the big shirt on **first**. The swim trunks are in the **middle**. I put the long pants on **last**.
• **left/right**	The slippers are on the **left** side of the shirt. The swimsuit is on the **right** end.
• **between**	Put the tennis shoes **between** the shirts.
• **before/after**	Put on the large shirt **before** the small shirt. **After** you put on the small button, put on the large button.
• **same/different**	The pants have the **same** number of pockets. The socks are **different** colors.
• **all/some/none**	**All** of the shirts have buttons. **Some** of the clothes are for boys only. **None** of the shoes have high heels.

Unit 4
Blooming Category Activities

Clothing

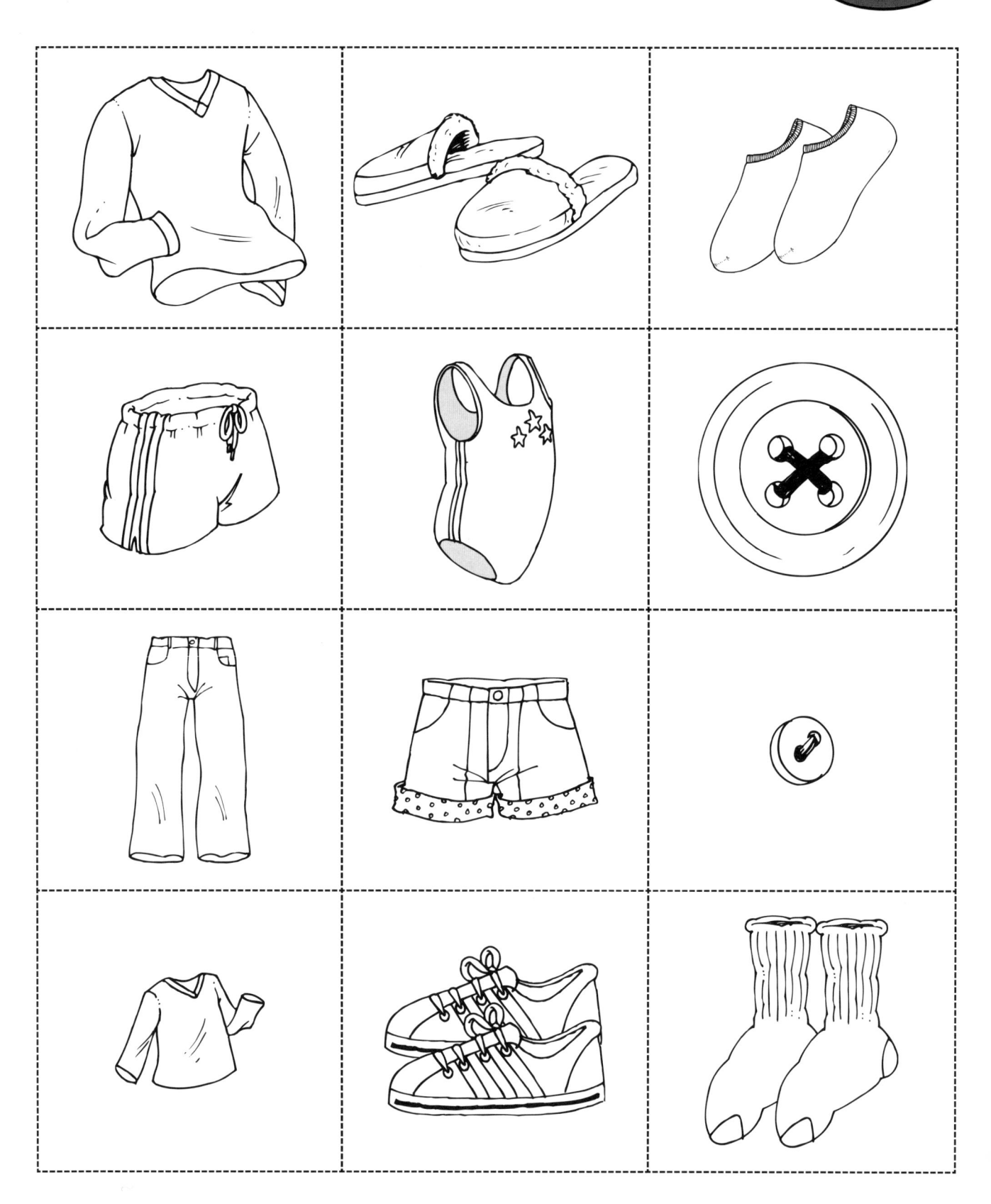

Concepts, *cont.*

Unit 4
Blooming Category Activities

Clothing

Bloom's Taxonomy

Objective: The child will answer increasingly more difficult questions about clothing based on *Bloom's Taxonomy of Educational Objectives*.

Ask these questions while doing the Dressing a Doll activity on page 43 and throughout all the activities in this lesson.

Knowledge
- Who wears a skirt?
- Where do you put dirty clothes?
- Count the buttons on the doll's clothes.
- Name three pieces of clothing.

Comprehension
- Tell how we dressed the doll.
- Describe a piece of clothing by using color, size, and texture adjectives.
- Compare a sweater and shirt.
- Match the doll's clothes to your clothes.

Application
- Tell how you get dressed in the morning.
- Name other clothes we could put on the doll.
- Sort the doll's clothes into dress clothes and play clothes.
- What happens if your shirt is missing a button?

Analysis
- How are pants and shorts alike? How are they different?
- In summer you wear a swimsuit. In winter you wear a _____.
- The sweater is soft. What is the opposite of *soft*?
- Tell the first and last clothing items we put on the doll.

Synthesis
- Draw a picture of your favorite outfit.
- What would it be like if it was cold and you did not have a coat?
- What would happen if your clothes were too small?
- Think of all the ways you can dress to keep warm.

Evaluation
- Did you like to dress the doll? Why?
- Would it work to wear your shorts to swim? Why?
- Your clothes from last year don't fit you any longer. Why?

Around the Home

Project

Playing With a Dollhouse

Materials:
- dollhouse
- dollhouse furniture

Directions:
- Play with a dollhouse and dollhouse furniture.
- Name all of the rooms in the dollhouse.
- Name all of the furniture for the dollhouse.
- Categorize the furniture by rooms and put it in the dollhouse.
- Talk about the functions of the items in each room.
- Talk about the rooms and the furniture in the dollhouse and compare them to the child's own home.

Around the Home

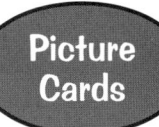

Picture Cards

➡ **Objective**: The child will increase receptive understanding and expressive use of vocabulary related to things around the home.

bathroom	bathtub	bed
bedroom	bookshelves	coffee table
dining room	dishes	dresser

Unit 5
Blooming Category Activities

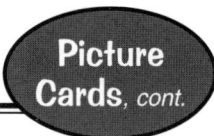

Around the Home

Picture Cards, cont.

family room	fork	garage
kitchen	lamp	mixer
nightstand	place mat	refrigerator

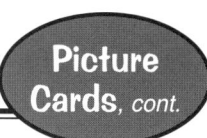

Around the Home

Picture Cards, *cont.*

remote control	sheets	shower
sink	sofa/couch	stove
tablecloth	television	toilet

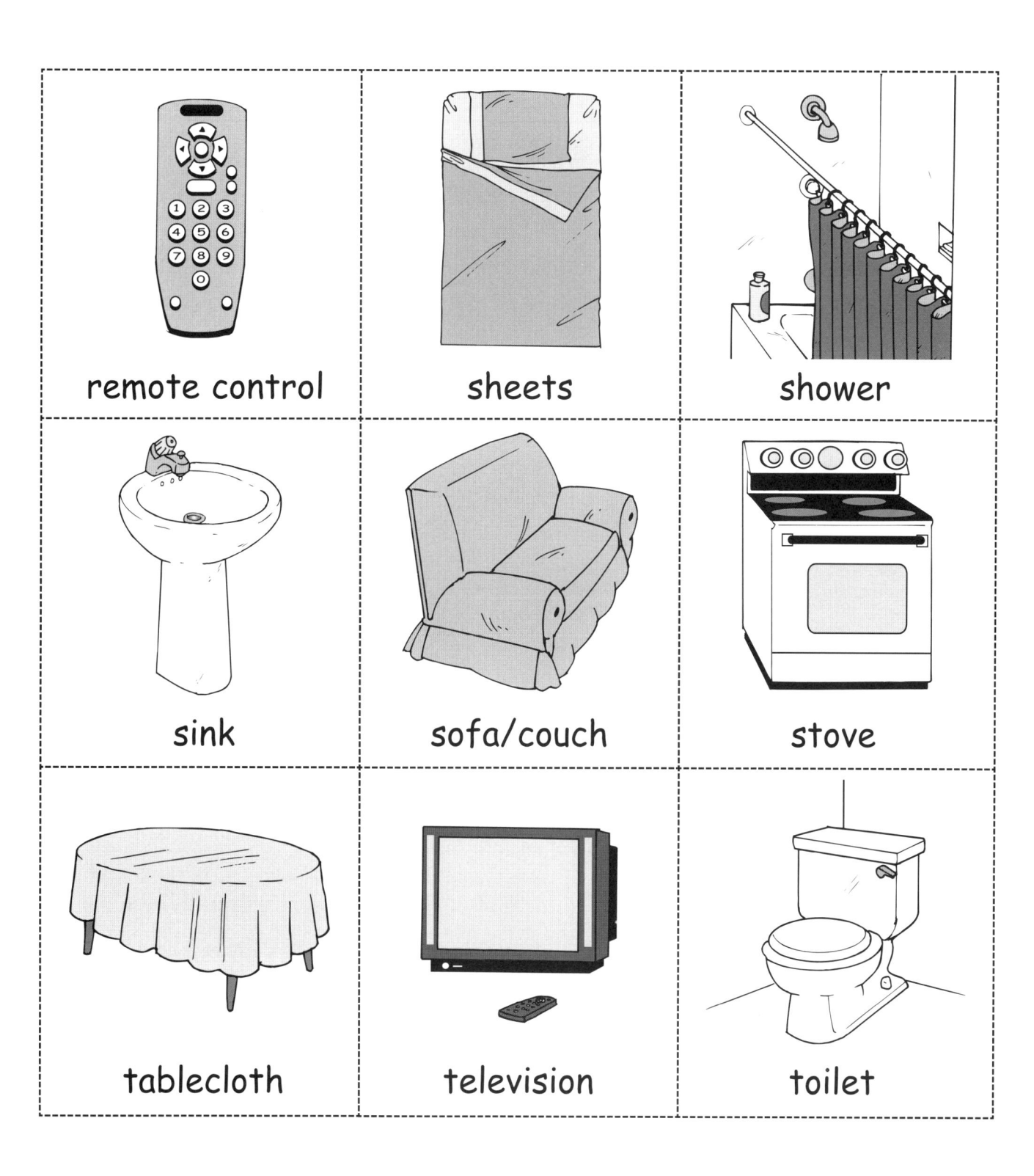

Around the Home

Family Letter

Dear Family,

In speech, we are learning about things in a home and the vocabulary that goes with that category. You can help your child practice this vocabulary at home. Talk about the picture below with your child and help her answer the questions. Then put this page up somewhere in your home to remind everyone to use "around the home" vocabulary with your child. Some suggestions to encourage this discussion are listed at the bottom of the page. Thank you,

_____

What room is this? Name all of the things you see in this picture that help you cook. Now name the items in your own kitchen.

- That's Dad's **recliner**.
- Put the milk in the **refrigerator**.
- My socks are in the top **dresser drawer**.
- I smell cookies baking in the **oven**.
- Put the dirty **silverware** in the **dishwasher**.

- Our **television** is in the **family room**.
- Wash your hair in the **shower**.
- I'll hang your coat in the **closet**.
- Is the car in the **garage**?
- Take the clothes out of the **dryer**.

Around the Home

Activities

For some of these activities, you will photocopy and cut apart the picture cards on pages 55-57.

- Have the child sort the picture cards by rooms and use sentences such as *A dresser goes in a bedroom.*

- After sorting the picture cards by rooms, have the child think of other items that could go in those rooms.

- Have each child draw or bring in a photograph of her home and tell about it.

- Have a child draw a picture card from a bag and act out the use of the room or object on the card. Let the other children guess what's on the card by using verbs to describe her actions. For instance, they might say, "She snores when she sleeps on the bed."

- Use a doll and bedroom items such as a crib, a blanket, and a pillow to encourage the child to use prepositional phrases in sentences. For example, the child might say, "The doll is under the blanket," or "Lay the doll's head on the pillow."

- Choose the cards that picture household items and tape them around the room. Let the child pretend to go shopping in a furniture or appliance store. As she decides what to buy, she can name it, tell what room it will go in, and say how she will use it.

- After looking at the cards that picture different rooms, let each child choose the room that is her favorite and tell why.

- Have the child use kitchen toys to name and describe the items needed and actions used to make a pretend sandwich.

- Bring in some common household cleaning items such as a mop, a broom, a cleaning cloth, and a dustpan. As the children pretend to clean a family room, have them name and describe the items they are "cleaning." Encourage the use of verbs such as *sweep*, *mop*, and *wipe*.

- Draw a large outline of a house on a poster board. Let the children take turns choosing a picture card, naming it, describing it, and gluing it in the correct room.

- Give the child two picture cards of items that would go in the same room, such as the dresser and the nightstand. Have her tell how the two items are the same and how they are different.

- Take an in-school field trip and name all of the furniture and appliances that you see. Talk about which ones could also be in a home and what rooms they would go in.

Around the Home

Objective: The child will use at least three components to define words related to items in a home.

Make a copy of this page and page 61. As you point to each picture, say the following prompts and fill in the chart with your students' answers. First, say, "Name this picture." Then, say, "Tell me a word that describes a/an _____." Next, ask, "What group does _____ belong to?" Finally, say, "Now let's put all the words together in a sentence to make a good definition of _____."

	Name	Describing Word	Group	Function
	spoon	round	silverware	eat soup with it

Unit 5
Blooming Category Activities

Around the Home

Worksheet, *cont.*

Name	Describing Word	Group	Function

Unit 5
Blooming Category Activities

Around the Home

Concepts

Objective: The child will demonstrate receptive understanding and expressive use of basic concepts while completing the activity.

Build a House

Materials:
- photocopies of pages 63 and 64 for each child
- scissors
- crayons or markers
- glue
- large sheet of construction paper

Directions:
- Draw or let the child draw an outline of the front of a house on a large sheet of construction paper.
- Have the child color and cut out the pictures on pages 63 and 64.
- Using concept words, tell the child where to glue some of the items.
- Let the child decide where to glue the remaining items and have her describe where she puts them.
- Have the children compare what is the same and different about their finished pictures.

Suggested Concepts to Target:

• top/middle/bottom	I put the chimney on **top** of the house. Glue the door in the **middle** of the house. The flower box is on the **bottom** of the window.
• left/right	The **left** window has a blue curtain on it. The tree is to the **right** of the house.
• next to/beside	Put the bush **next to** the door. The tree is **beside** the house.
• before/after	**Before** you glue on the windows, put on the door. What did you put on **after** the chimney?
• front/back	This is the **front** of the house. There is a yard in **back** of the house.
• same/different	We made our doors the **same** color. This house is **different** from my house.
• above/below	Put a window **above** the door. The flower box is **below** the window.
• between	The door is **between** two windows.
• all/some/none	**All** of the windows have curtains. **Some** of this house is like mine. **None** of the windows are open.

Unit 5
Blooming Category Activities

Around the Home

Concepts, cont.

Unit 5
Blooming Category Activities

Around the Home

Concepts, *cont.*

Around the Home

Bloom's Taxonomy

→ **Objective**: The child will answer increasingly more difficult questions about things around the home based on *Bloom's Taxonomy of Educational Objectives*.

Ask these questions while doing the Playing With a Dollhouse activity on page 54 and throughout all of the activities in this lesson.

Knowledge
- Name three kinds of furniture you put in the dollhouse.
- How many rooms are in the dollhouse?
- Where did you put the table?
- Name the furniture in the bedroom.

Comprehension
- What kind of furniture goes with a table?
- Draw a picture of your home.
- Describe your bed.
- Explain why you need an oven in the kitchen.

Application
- Put all of the chairs in the living/family room.
- Where would you sleep if you didn't have a bed?
- What's another name for a *sofa*?
- Name some other furniture you could have put in the family room.

Analysis
- How is your home like your next-door neighbor's home?
- How is a high chair different from a rocking chair?
- You sleep in a bed. You eat at a _____.
- What did you put in the dollhouse first? What is the last thing you put in the dollhouse?

Synthesis
- Create a brand new kind of room for your home. What would be in it?
- Think of all the things you could cook in an oven.
- What would it be like if you didn't have a home to live in?
- Tell a good definition of the word *furniture*.

Evaluation
- What is the most useful kitchen appliance? Why?
- What is your favorite room in your home? Why?
- Do you like a regular oven or a microwave oven better? Why?

Day and Night

Project

Playing with Dolls

Materials:
- doll or stuffed animal
- doll toys such as a bed, a blanket, and a pillow
- bedtime storybook
- cereal, bowl, spoon
- cup
- alarm clock
- daytime and nighttime clothes for the doll

Directions:
- Play with the doll or stuffed animal.
- Pretend that it is nighttime and talk about the child's nighttime routine.
- Dress the doll in pajamas, read it a bedtime story, and put it to bed.
- Pretend that it is daytime and talk about the child's morning routine.
- Set the alarm clock for the doll to wake up.
- Pretend to stretch and wake up.
- Share some cereal.
- Dress the doll in clothes for the day.
- Talk about all of the things the child can do during the daytime.

Day and Night

Picture Cards

➤ **Objective:** The child will increase receptive understanding and expressive use of vocabulary related to day and night.

alarm clock	blanket	breakfast
dew	dream	dress
hairbrush	mirror	moon

Unit 6
Blooming Category Activities

Day and Night

Picture Cards, cont.

morning	nightgown	night-light
nighttime	pajamas	pillow
shadow	sleep	snore

Unit 6
Blooming Category Activities

Day and Night

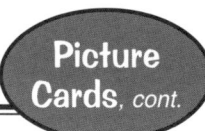

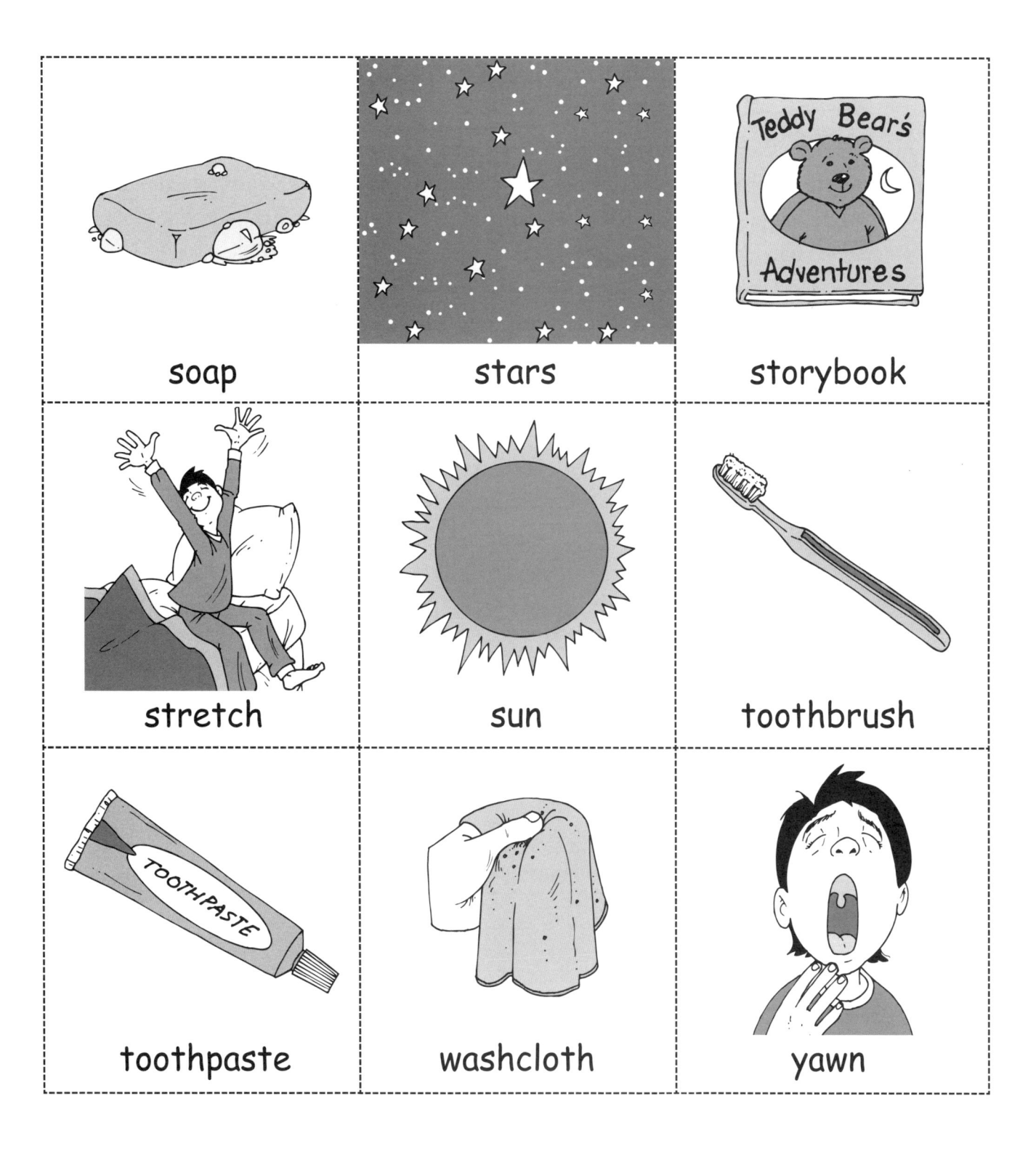

Picture Cards, cont.

soap	stars	storybook
stretch	sun	toothbrush
toothpaste	washcloth	yawn

Unit 6
Blooming Category Activities

Day and Night

Family Letter

Dear Family,

In speech, we are learning about day and night and the vocabulary that goes with this category, such as things in the sky (the moon or a rainbow), daytime or nighttime activities, or your child's routine of going to bed and waking up. You can help your child practice this vocabulary at home. Talk about the picture below with your child and help him use the target words. Then put this page somewhere in your home to remind everyone to talk about day and night. Some other suggestions to encourage this practice are included at the bottom of this page. Thank you, _____

Tell about this picture. What time of day is it? What do you eat for breakfast?

- My **bed** is big.
- I set the **alarm clock** at **night**.
- My dad **snores**.
- Put on your **pajamas**.
- I **wake up** at 7 o'clock.

- I **yawn** when I am **sleepy**.
- My mom **sleeps** with two **pillows**.
- There was a **full moon** last **night**.
- I saw the **sun rise** this **morning**.
- On a **sunny day**, I can see my **shadow**.

Unit 6
Blooming Category Activities

Day and Night

Activities

For some of these activities, you will photocopy and cut apart the picture cards on pages 67-69.

- Recite poems or sing songs such as "Star Light, Star Bright," "Twinkle, Twinkle Little Star," and "Good Morning to You."

- Talk about animals that are active at night, such as *owls*, *bats*, *raccoons*, and *mice*.

- Give each child three sheets of paper: a black one for night, a blue one for day, and a yellow one to represent both day and night. Let the child choose a picture card, name it, and then put it on the black paper if it is a picture associated with night, on the blue paper if it is associated with day, or on the yellow paper if it is something that can be associated with both day and night.

- Read the book "Good Night Moon" and practice saying "good night" to all of the items in the book.

- Give each child two paper plates, one for dinner and one for breakfast. Let the child draw or cut out pictures from a grocery ad or magazine and glue them on the plates. Discuss food that you would typically eat in the daytime or at night. You can also talk about some foods that are appropriate for both.

- Tape the picture cards around the room. Turn off the lights so that the room is dark. Let the child use a flashlight to search for the picture cards. When he shines the light on a picture, take it off the wall. Continue until he has found all the pictures. Then have the child name and talk about the pictures.

- Put the picture cards in a pillowcase. Have the children take turns pulling a card out, naming it, and talking about if it is associated with day, night, or both.

- Choose the picture cards that are made up of two words (compound words). Talk about what the two words mean when they are separate and then about what they mean when they are put together.

- Turn on a flashlight or lamp that allows you to direct the light. Then turn off the other lights in the room. Talk about sunlight, darkness, shadows, daytime, and nighttime. Let the children use cutouts of pictures, or their hands to make shadow pictures on the wall.

- Let the child cut out and glue a large yellow circle in the middle of a poster board. This will represent the sun. Then have the child name the picture cards and glue them in rows coming out from the sun to represent the sun's rays.

- Get at least 20 index cards or pieces of paper and write *day* on half of them and *night* on the other half. Mix them up. Then let the children take turns choosing a card. If the card says *day*, the child must name an activity he could do in the daytime. If the card says *night*, he must name a nighttime activity.

- Choose selected picture cards and put them into an empty cereal box. Let the children take turns choosing a card out of the box and then acting out the picture. Have the other children try to guess the picture.

Unit 6
Blooming Category Activities

Day and Night

Worksheet

➡ **Objective:** The child will increase receptive understanding and expressive use of vocabulary related to day and night while discussing inconsistencies in a "What's Wrong?" picture.

Photocopy the picture below for each child. Discuss the picture and talk about the child's own bedtime routine. Next, let the child find and circle all of the absurdities or inconsistencies in the picture. Then have him tell about each "wrong thing" he found in the picture and how he would make it right.

Unit 6
Blooming Category Activities

Day and Night

Concepts

➡ **Objective**: The child will demonstrate receptive understanding and expressive use of basic concepts while ordering and telling sequence stories based on day and night.

Day and Night Sequence Stories

Materials:
- a photocopy of page 74 for each child
- crayons or markers
- scissors
- two sheets of construction paper for each child, one black and one blue

Directions:
- Color and cut out the pictures on page 74.
- Find three pictures that tell a nighttime story.
- Find three pictures that tell a daytime story.
- Glue the nighttime story pictures in order on the black paper.
- Glue the daytime story pictures in order on the blue paper.
- Tell each story with your best speech.

Suggested Concepts to Target:

- **all/some/none** — **All** of the pictures have children in them. **Some** of the pictures have a girl in them. **None** of the pictures have a monkey in them.

- **first/last** — **First** they cooked marshmallows. The **last** thing they did was sleep.

- **left/right** — Point to the picture that is on the **left**. Color the picture on the **right**.

- **before/after** — What did she do **before** she got on the bus? What do you do **after** you get dressed?

- **beside/between** — The dog is **beside** the mom. The girl is sitting **between** the boys.

- **alike/different** — These pictures are **alike** because they all are at night. Our school bus is **different** from that one.

- **in/on** — The moon is **in** the sky. The owl is sitting **on** a branch.

- **over/under** — Her backpack is **over** her shoulder. What is **under** her hand?

- **long/tall** — The school bus is **long**. That tree is **tall**.

- **whole/part** — Tell me the **whole** story. Tell me the last **part** of the story.

Day and Night

Concepts, cont.

Unit 6
Blooming Category Activities

Day and Night

Bloom's Taxonomy

→ **Objective**: The child will answer increasingly more difficult questions about day and night based on *Bloom's Taxonomy of Educational Objectives*.

Ask these questions while doing the Playing with Dolls activity on page 66 and throughout all of the activities in this lesson.

Knowledge
- Where did you put the pillow?
- Name three things we used when we played with the doll.
- What room is your bed in?
- Who helps you get ready for bed?

Comprehension
- Tell how we played with the doll.
- Describe your bedroom.
- Explain what you do when you get up in the morning.
- What does the word *night* mean?

Application
- What else goes on your bed besides your pillow?
- Name some other things you can sleep on besides a bed.
- How could you keep warm at night if you didn't have a blanket?
- What's another word for *slippers*?

Analysis
- I wake up in the morning. I go to bed at _____.
- What's the opposite of *awake*?
- How are the sun and the moon alike?
- How are a yawn and a stretch different?

Synthesis
- What if you went to your friend's house to sleep and you forgot your toothbrush?
- Create a bedtime story you would like to hear.
- Think of all the foods you could eat for breakfast.
- What would it be like if you decided to sleep outside?

Evaluation
- Would you rather wake up or go to bed? Why?
- You're outside, but you can't see your shadow. Why?
- Would you rather sleep with a light on or with all the lights off? Why?

Occupations

Project

Matching Objects to Occupations

Materials:
- copy of the occupation picture cards on pages 77-79
- objects or pictures of objects that are associated with each occupation such as *hammer* and *carpenter*, *stethoscope* and *doctor*, *mixing bowl* and *chef*, etc.

Directions:
- Cut apart the picture cards.
- Put the picture cards in a bag or in a stack on the table.
- Place the objects or pictures of associated objects around the room.
- Let a child choose a picture and name the occupation.
- Have the child find and name an object that goes with the pictured occupation.
- Have the child tell how the worker uses that object.
- When working with a group, one child can name the occupation picture, one can find the matching object, and another can tell how they go together.

Occupations

Picture Cards

➡️ **Objective**: The child will increase receptive understanding and expressive use of vocabulary related to occupations.

artist	astronaut	barber
butcher	car mechanic	carpenter
chef	dentist	doctor

Unit 7
Blooming Category Activities

Occupations

Picture Cards, cont.

farmer	firefighter	judge
mail carrier	musician	nurse
optometrist	photographer	pilot

Unit 7
Blooming Category Activities

Occupations

Picture Cards, *cont.*

plumber	police officer	scientist
secretary	soldier	teacher
truck driver	veterinarian	waiter

Occupations

Family Letter

Dear Family,

In speech, we are learning about the vocabulary that goes with many different types of occupations. You can help your child practice this vocabulary at home. Talk about the picture below with your child and help her use occupation words to describe the picture and answer the questions. Then put this page somewhere in your home to help everyone remember to "get to work" on using occupation words. Some suggestions to encourage this are listed at the bottom of the page. Be sure to talk about the jobs held by the members of your family and the tools they use for those jobs.

Thank you, _____

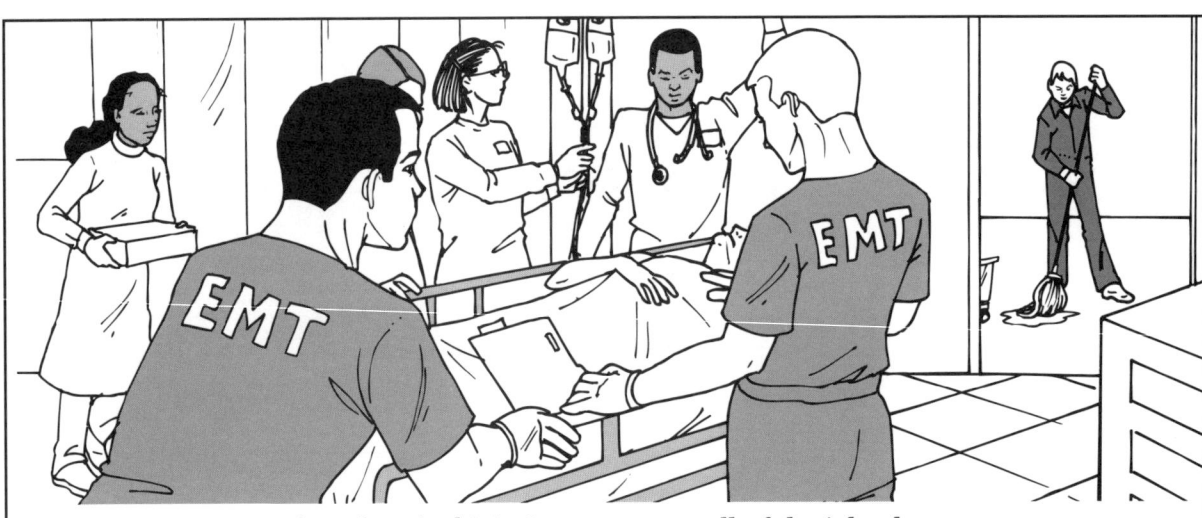

What place is this? Can you name all of the jobs that you see people doing? What other jobs could you have in a hospital?

- That **ambulance** is going to the **hospital**.
- Mom **works** downtown in an **office**.
- When I grow up I want to be a _____.
- I like my new **teacher**.
- Ask the **librarian** about that **book**.

- Smile for the **photographer**.
- She is my favorite **singer**.
- The **waitress** will take our **order**.
- Let's grow **vegetables** like a **farmer**.
- The **barber** cuts Dad's **hair**.

Unit 7
Blooming Category Activities
80
Copyright © 2006 LinguiSystems, Inc.

Occupations

Activities

For some of these activities, you will photocopy and cut apart the picture cards on pages 77-79.

- Have one child choose an occupation picture from a box and act it out while the other children guess the occupation and use verbs to describe the actions.

- While playing with toy vehicles or looking at pictures of them, have the child tell about the kinds of jobs that go with each vehicle.

- Have the child choose a picture card and name where that person would work. For example, she might say, "A chef works in a restaurant" or "A butcher works in a grocery store or a meat market."

- Let the child pretend to be a chef and bake a cake. Encourage her to use verbs such as *measure, mix, stir, cook, smell, pour,* and *eat*.

- Let the child paint a picture with watercolors while pretending to be an artist. Encourage her to use color and size adjectives as well as other descriptive adjectives, such as *wet, dry,* and *pretty*.

- Let the child act out different occupations while singing "This is the Way." For example, she might sing, "This is the way you put out a fire, put out a fire, put out a fire. This is the way you put out a fire when you are a firefighter" while pretending to hold a fire hose.

- Have the child sort the picture cards into those occupations that wear uniforms and those that do not.

- Lay the occupation picture cards on the table. Have each child tell the three jobs she would most like to do and why.

- Let the child pretend to be a postal worker. Encourage the child to use sentences containing prepositional phrases, such as *I put the stamp on the envelope, I wrote the address under the name, I put the letter in the envelope,* and *I wear the mailbag over my shoulder*.

- Let the child use a toy doctor's kit and pretend to take care of a "sick" doll. Encourage her to use verbs, such as *hold, fix, heal, wrap,* and *stick*; prepositional phrases, such as *under the arm, around the ankle,* and *on the hand*; and adjectives, such as *hot, hurt,* and *healthy*.

- Tape some of the occupation pictures on the wall. Give a clue about one of them, such as *This person uses a hammer*. If the child guesses the correct occupation, let her throw a bean bag or a foam ball and try to hit the correct picture.

- Put the occupation pictures on the floor around the room. Let the child pretend to be a truck driver. Have her drive to each picture, stop on it, and tell something about it.

- Have each child tell about the jobs held by members of her family.

- Categorize the picture cards into jobs that are done outside and those that are done inside.

Occupations

Worksheet

→ **Objective**: The child will match occupations with associated items and use verbs to tell what the person does with the object.

Have the child name the job shown in the target picture. Then have her name the three objects in the row beside that picture. Tell her to circle the object that goes with the job. Finally, have her say a sentence that tells what that person does with the object. (The sentence can be present tense: "A farmer can dig up dirt with a shovel," third person singular: "The barber cuts hair with scissors," present progressive: "The scientist is looking in a microscope," or past tense: "The photographer took my picture with a camera.")

Unit 7
Blooming Category Activities

82

Copyright © 2006 LinguiSystems, Inc.

Occupations

Concepts

➡ **Objective**: The child will demonstrate receptive understanding and expressive use of basic concepts while completing the activity.

Mail Time

Materials:
- a photocopy of the shapes on page 84 for each child
- scissors
- crayons or markers
- shoebox with lid
- stickers or stamps
- small envelopes

Directions: Follow the directions on page 84 to make "letters" and mail them.

Suggested Concepts to Target:

- **first/last**   Color the oval **first**.
                              Mail the small rectangle **last**.

- **small/large**   Cut out the **small** oval.
                              Mail the **large** rectangle.

- **in/out**   Put the shape **in** the envelope.
                              Take the envelope **out** of the mailbox.

- **on/off**   Put a sticker **on** the small oval.
                              Take the top **off** of the mailbox.

- **before/after**   Color the large oval **before** you cut it out.
                              Seal the envelope **after** you put the shape in it.

- **left/right**   Write your name in the **left** corner.
                              Put the stamp in the **right** corner.

- **front/back**   The sticker goes on the **front** of the envelope.
                              You lick the **back** of the envelope.

- **center/corner**   Write your name in the **center**.
                              Put a stamp in the **corner**.

Occupations

Concepts, *cont.*

Directions:
- Let the child color and cut out these shapes.
- Cut a slit in the lid of the shoebox that is big enough to put an envelope through.
- Tell the child to choose a shape, describe it by size and color, and put it in an envelope.
- Give the child instructions on decorating the envelope with crayons or stickers.
- Let the child mail the envelope by dropping it through the slit into the shoebox.

Unit 7
Blooming Category Activities

Occupations

Bloom's Taxonomy

→ **Objective**: The child will answer increasingly more difficult questions about occupations based on *Bloom's Taxonomy of Educational Objectives*.

Ask these questions while doing the Matching Objects to Occupations activity on page 76 and throughout all of the activities in this lesson.

Knowledge
- Name one job we talked about.
- What job goes with a hammer?
- Name three jobs you could have in a hospital.
- Where does a chef work?

Comprehension
- Tell what a teacher does.
- Give an example of two occupations that are done outside.
- What is the main duty of a police officer?
- Explain why you go to the doctor.

Application
- What is another word for *occupation*?
- What other objects could we bring to match with these occupation pictures?
- Have you ever had a job? Tell about it.
- What's wrong with a pilot who is afraid of heights?

Analysis
- An engineer drives a train. A paramedic drives an _____.
- Why does a doctor need to go to school for so many years?
- How are an artist and a photographer alike?
- How are a pilot and an astronaut different?

Synthesis
- Suppose you become a police officer. What would you want to do first?
- Pretend that your job is the mayor. How would you improve your city?
- Create a brand new occupation for the future and tell about it.
- Predict what would happen if all of the teachers quit their jobs.

Evaluation
- Which job is your favorite one? Why?
- Would you rather work inside or outside? Why?
- Would you rather be a veterinarian or a doctor? Why?

Transportation

Project

Categorizing Vehicles by Land, Air, and Sea

Materials:
- copy of the transportation picture cards on pages 87-89
- large sheet of paper or poster board
- glue or tape

Directions:
- Draw the sky, a body of water, a road, a sidewalk, and a train track on the poster board.
- Put the poster on the table or attach it to the wall.
- Talk about the areas of land, sky, and water on the poster.
- Let each child take a turn choosing one of the picture cards and naming it.
- Have the child use glue or tape to attach the picture card to the appropriate place on the poster.
- Talk about each vehicle. Tell how it moves and what its purpose is.
- Let the children try to think of other vehicles that could go on the land, in the air, or on the water.

Transportation

Picture Cards

Objective: The child will increase receptive understanding and expressive use of transportation vocabulary.

18-wheeler	airplane	bicycle
bus	canoe	car
convertible	headlights	helicopter

Unit 8
Blooming Category Activities

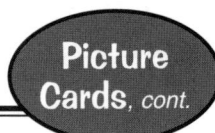

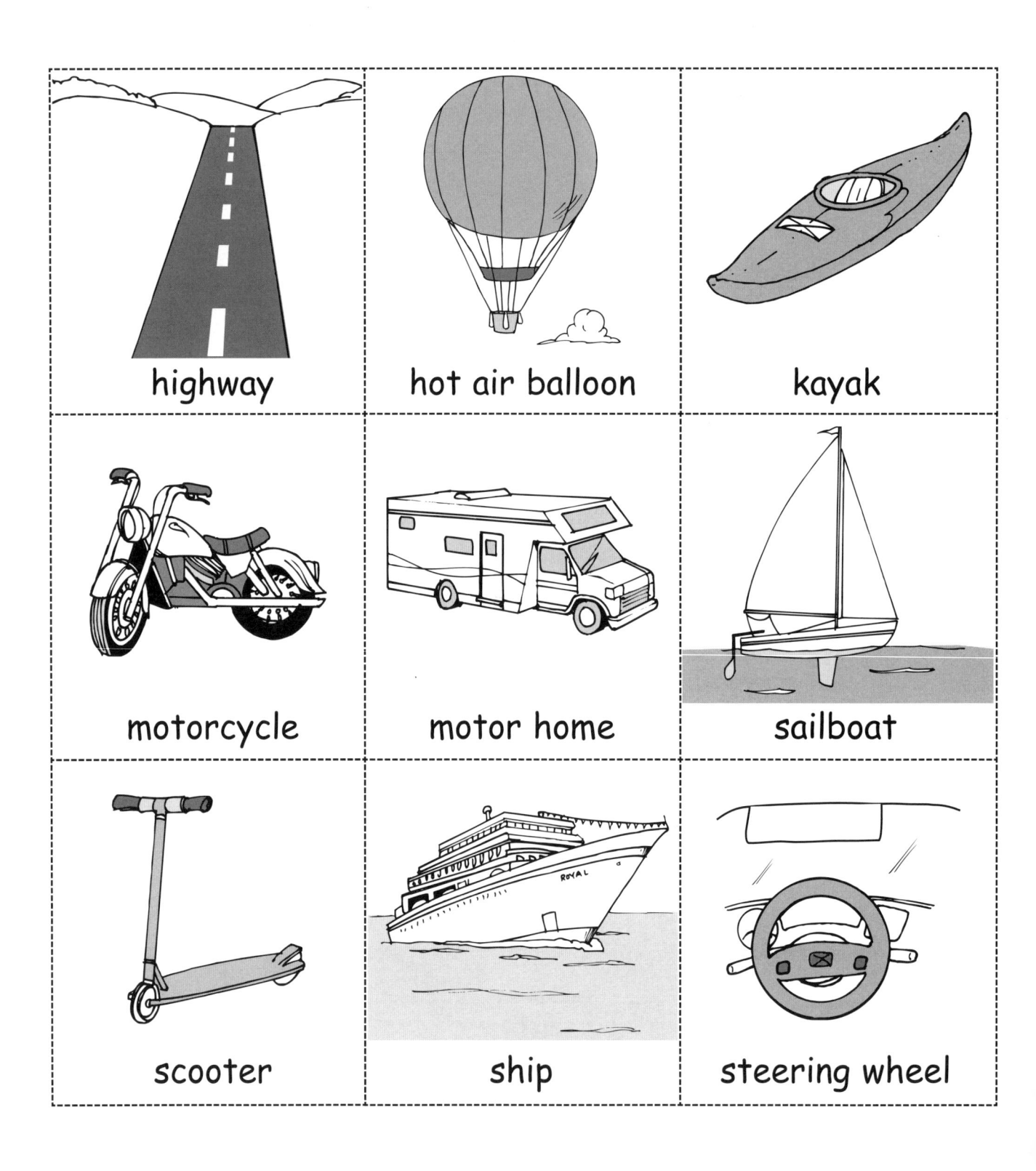

Transportation

Picture Cards, cont.

highway	hot air balloon	kayak
motorcycle	motor home	sailboat
scooter	ship	steering wheel

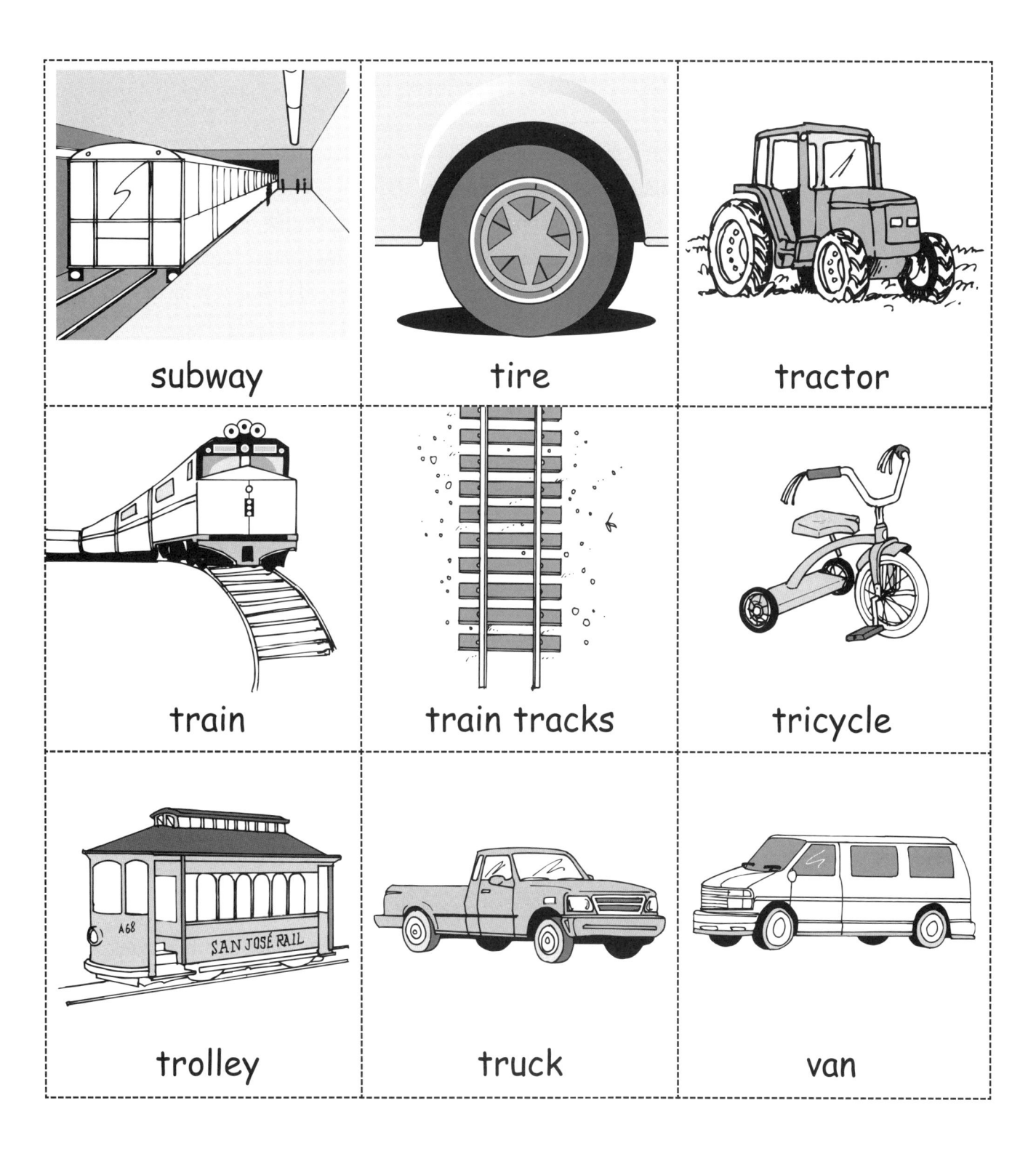

Transportation

Picture Cards, cont.

subway	tire	tractor
train	train tracks	tricycle
trolley	truck	van

Unit 8
Blooming Category Activities 89 Copyright © 2006 LinguiSystems, Inc.

Transportation

Family Letter

Dear Family,

In speech, we are learning all about transportation and the vocabulary that goes with that category. You can help your child practice this vocabulary at home. Talk about the picture below with your child and help him use transportation words to answer the questions. Then put this page in a high traffic area in your home or in the car to remind everyone to help your child talk about transportation. Some ideas to encourage this are listed at the bottom of the page. Thank you, _____

Have you ever been to an airport? Tell about the transportation items you see in this airport. Which one is your favorite?

- Mom drives a **van**.
- Dad rides a **subway** to work.
- Always **buckle** your **seat belt**.
- We rode a **bus** on our school field trip.
- Wear a **helmet** when you ride your **bicycle**.

- I ride my **scooter** on the **sidewalk**.
- Let's count the **wheels** on that big **truck**.
- How many **cars** are on that **train**?
- That farmer has a **tractor**.
- I hear the **siren** from the **fire truck**.

Unit 8
Blooming Category Activities 90 Copyright © 2006 LinguiSystems, Inc.

Transportation

Activities

For some of these activities, you will photocopy and cut apart the picture cards on pages 87-89.

- Let each child pull one of the picture cards out of a bag and act it out. The other children will guess the transportation word.

- Stand in a row and pretend to be on a train or a bus ride. Let the children follow instructions such as *stop, go, slow, fast, over, under, around, forward,* and *backward*.

- Decorate small gift boxes or shoeboxes to look like train cars and then fill them with different kinds of "cargo" such as *cotton balls, rocks,* and *toothpicks*. Have the children use shape, size, texture, and other descriptive adjectives to describe the cargo.

- Let each child describe an object as the children take turns packing a suitcase to take on a trip.

- While playing with toy vehicles, help the children describe them by size, speed, noise, color, texture, shape, and function.

- Sing "The Wheels on the Bus."

- Let each child choose one of the picture cards out of the back of a toy truck and make the noise associated with that vehicle. Have the other children guess the noise and name the picture.

- Have races with toy cars and encourage use of the words *first, middle, last, fast, slow, stop,* and *go*.

- While looking at the picture cards or transportation toys, have the children count and name the parts on the vehicles.

- Use some of the transportation picture cards to make a game board. After rolling a die, let the child move a toy car that number of spaces. Then have him name and describe the picture he lands on.

- Sing "Row, Row, Row Your Boat."

- Ask each child to bring or draw a picture of his family's transportation and tell about it.

- Let a child choose two picture cards or toy vehicles and tell how they are the same and how they are different.

Transportation

Worksheet

▶ **Objective:** The child will increase his understanding and use of comparatives and superlatives while describing pictures of vehicles.

Name the three types of transportation in each row. Use the target word in the column on the left to describe the three pictures. Tell about each picture using the target word, the target word + **er**, or the target word + **est**. (The pictures are not always in the correct order.)

1. fast	motorcycle	bicycle	space shuttle
2. loud	bicycle	truck	airplane
3. long	train	bus	van
4. small	canoe	skateboard	sailboat
5. slow	hot air balloon	tractor	tricycle

Unit 8
Blooming Category Activities
Copyright © 2006 LinguiSystems, Inc.

Transportation

Concepts

▶ **Objective:** The child will demonstrate receptive understanding and expressive use of basic concepts while completing the activity.

Shape Train

Materials:
- a photocopy of page 94 for each child
- scissors
- crayons or markers

Directions:
- Let the child color the engine, caboose, and shapes on page 94.
- Cut out or have the child cut out the pictures.
- Have the child make a train. Tell him to put the engine first and the caboose last. Explain that he will use the shapes for the cars in the middle.
- Tell the child where to put each shape car, using concept words such as *between*, *to the left*, *beside*, *next to*, etc.
- Let the child use concept words to tell where specific train cars are located.

Suggested Concepts to Target:

- **first/last**
  Put the engine **first**.
  The caboose is **last**.

- **left/right**
  Put the square to the **left** of a circle.
  The blue triangle is to the **right** of the red triangle.

- **big/small**
  The purple circle is **big**.
  Color the **small** square yellow.

- **next to/beside**
  The square is **next to** the engine.
  Put the circle **beside** the caboose.

- **same/different**
  Our trains are the **same** size.
  Our trains are **different** colors.

- **equal/more/less**
  These trains have an **equal** number of cars.
  Her train has **more** blue cars.
  A car is **less** noisy than a motorcycle.

- **on/off**
  Put your train **on** a track.
  Take the caboose **off** of your train.

- **before/after**
  Color the shapes **before** you make the train.
  Cut out the shapes **after** you color them.

Unit 8
Blooming Category Activities

Transportation

Concepts, *cont.*

Unit 8
Blooming Category Activities

Transportation

Bloom's Taxonomy

→ **Objective**: The child will answer increasingly more difficult questions about transportation based on *Bloom's Taxonomy of Educational Objectives*.

Ask these questions while doing the Categorizing Vehicles by Land, Air, and Sea activity on page 86 and throughout all of the activities in this lesson.

Knowledge
- How many vehicles did you put in the water?
- Where did you put the airplane?
- When you finished the picture, did you have more items on the land, in the air, or on the water?
- Who flies an airplane?

Comprehension
- Draw a picture of a boat.
- Describe a vehicle you put on the land.
- Match these toy vehicles with the picture cards we used.
- How did we make the picture?

Application
- Tell about the kind of transportation you used to get here today.
- Look at the vehicles you put on the land. Name some other vehicles that could go on the land.
- What's another name for *airplane*?
- What's wrong with sailing a boat on a road?

Analysis
- How are a plane and a helicopter alike?
- How are a train and a bus different?
- What makes a sailboat move?
- A car goes on a road. A train goes on _____.

Synthesis
- What is something else we could have done with the picture cards?
- Design your own rocket ship.
- Suppose your car ran out of gas. What would you do?
- Pretend you are going on a trip around the world. Name all the kinds of transportation you would use.

Evaluation
- What is your favorite kind of transportation? Why?
- Would you rather travel on the land, in the air, or on the water? Why?
- What would be the best kind of transportation in the jungle? Why?

Toys

Project

Making Play Putty

Materials:
- liquid starch
- glue
- bowl for mixing
- measuring cup
- spoon

Directions:
- Measure equal parts of the liquid starch and glue.
- Use a spoon to mix the two together.
- Knead the putty until it's smooth.
- Play and enjoy!

While doing the activity, mention various concepts, such as:
- **First** measure the glue, **then** measure the starch.
- Pour the glue **into** the bowl.
- Tell me what you did **first**.
- Where did you put the starch?
- What was the **last** thing you did?

Toys

Picture Cards

⇨ **Objective**: The child will increase receptive understanding and expressive use of toys vocabulary.

airplane	balloon	blocks
blow	bubbles	catch
doll	dollhouse	drum

Unit 9
Blooming Category Activities

Toys

Picture Cards, cont.

football	game	kite
marbles	paint	puppet
puzzle	rattle	rocking horse

Unit 9
Blooming Category Activities

Toys

Picture Cards, cont.

roll	stack	tea set
teddy bear	throw	toy box
train	truck	whistle

Toys

Family Letter

Dear Family,

In speech, we are learning about toys and the vocabulary that goes with that category. You can help your child practice this vocabulary at home. Talk about the picture below with your child and help her use toy words to answer the questions. Then put this page in a high traffic area in your home to remind everyone to help your child talk about toys. Some ideas to encourage this are listed at the bottom of the page.

Thank you, _____

These children are at school. Name the toys you see. What is your favorite center at school?

- Name all the **toys** in this picture.
- I put my **toys** in the **toy box**.
- I got a new **puzzle** for my birthday.
- We **blew bubbles**.
- We like to **fly kites** on windy days.

- Dad and I **play catch** with my **football**.
- He collects **toy trains**.
- Do not **throw** your **teddy bear**.
- She can **stack** the **blocks**.
- The baby likes the **rocking horse**.

Unit 9
Blooming Category Activities

Toys

Activities

For some of these activities, you will photocopy and cut apart the picture cards on pages 97-99.

- Put the picture cards around the room to create a toy store. Let the child use play money to buy items in the toy store. Then have her name and describe each toy she bought.

- Ask each child to bring her favorite toy for Show and Tell. Have her bring it in a bag so the other children cannot see it. Have the child give clues about the toy's size, color, shape, and texture. Let the other children guess what the toy is.

- Put sand in a large container. Bury the picture cards in the sand. Have the child use a toy shovel to dig for the pictures. When she finds a picture, have the child say the name of the toy.

- Put the picture cards in a pile. The child selects a picture, names the picture, and tells if it is an inside or outside toy.

- Place the picture cards in a circle on the floor. Have the children sit behind the cards to form another circle. Let the children roll a ball back and forth. When a child rolls the ball over a picture, have her name the toy on the picture and tell what she would do with it.

- Have the child name a toy and then bounce a ball to a friend. That child names another toy and bounces the ball to another child.

- Use old magazines and catalogs. Let the child cut out pictures from the magazines and create a toy collage. Have her name and describe each picture she adds to the collage.

- Fold up the picture cards and slide them into balloons. Inflate the balloons and put them around the room. Let the child pop the balloons, one at a time, naming the picture in the balloon.

- Put a paper clip on each picture. Make a fishing pole by tying a piece of yarn to the end of a stick or yardstick. Tie a magnet on the other end of the yarn. Spread the picture cards out on the floor. Let the child go "fishing." Have her use shape, size, and color adjectives to describe each picture she "catches."

Toys

Worksheet

➤ **Objective:** The child will increase receptive knowledge and expressive use of verbs.

Photocopy this page for each child. Have the child name all of the toys and all of the verbs. Then have the child draw a line from each verb to the toy that goes with it. Ask the child to use the name of the toy and its matching verb in a sentence.

Unit 9
Blooming Category Activities

Toys

Concepts

➡ **Objective**: The child will demonstrate receptive understanding and expressive use of basic concepts while completing the activity.

Toy Room

Materials:
- glue stick
- scissors
- photocopies of pages 104-105 for each child

Directions:
- Have the child name all of the toys.
- Have the child color the toys and cut them out.
- Let the child glue the toys onto the playroom picture following directions with different concepts.

Suggested Concepts to Target:

- **left/right** Glue the car on the **left** side of the toy box.
  Put the rocking horse on the **right** side of the room.

- **in/on** Glue the ball **in** the toy box.
  Put the puzzle **on** the table.

- **next to/beside** Glue the teddy bear **next to** the rocking horse.
  Glue the train **beside** the airplane.

- **in front/behind** Put the airplane **in front** of the shelf.
  Put the doll **behind** the chair.

- **first/last** Glue the paints **first**.
  You glued the puzzle on **last**.

Toys

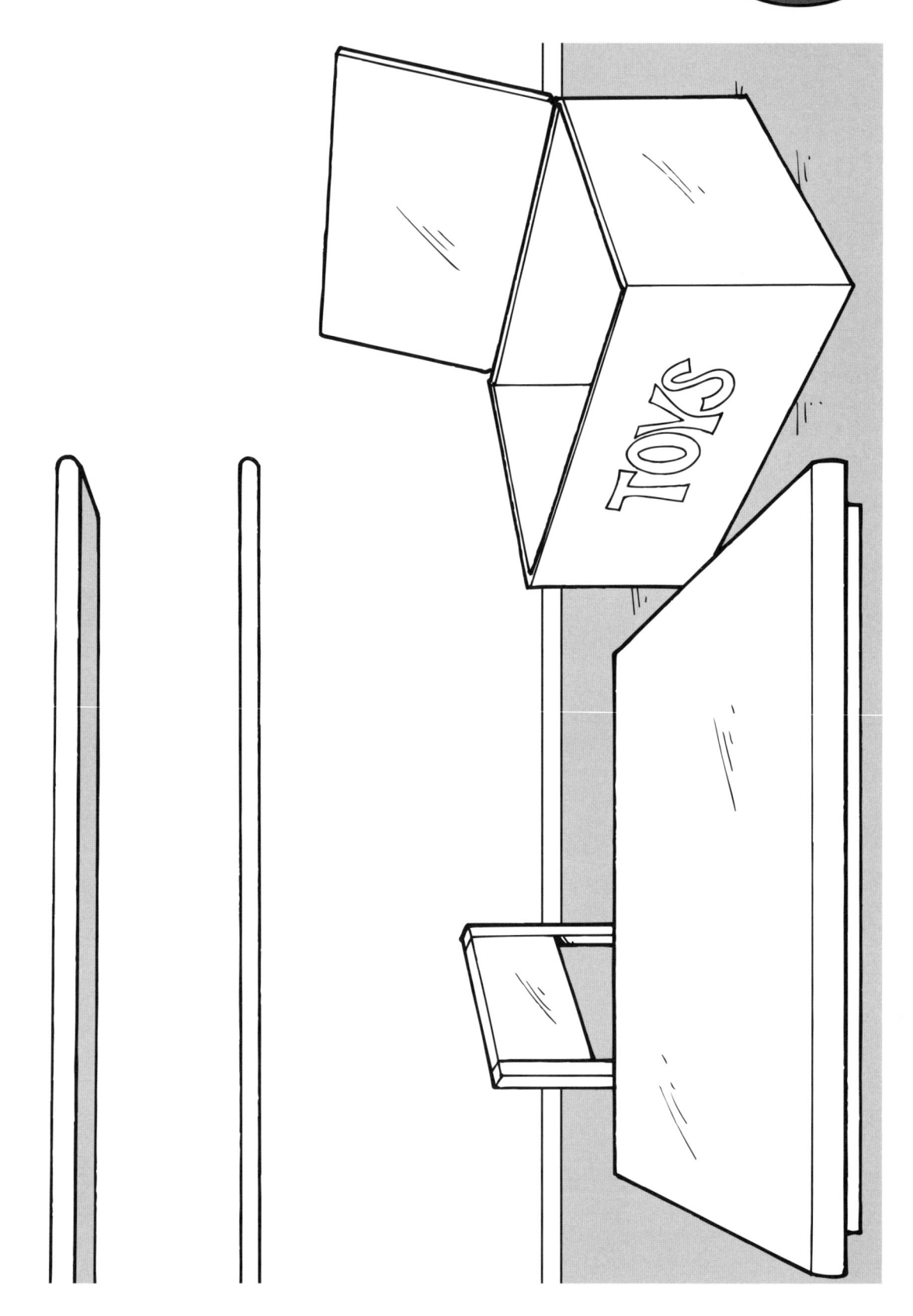

Concepts, *cont.*

Unit 9
Blooming Category Activities

Toys

Concepts, cont.

Toys

Bloom's Taxonomy

Objective: The child will answer increasingly more difficult questions about toys based on *Bloom's Taxonomy of Educational Objectives*.

Ask these questions while doing the Making Play Putty activity on page 96 and throughout all of the activities in this lesson.

Knowledge
- How many ingredients did we use to make the play putty?
- What did we make?
- Name three toys.
- Which toy can you catch?

Comprehension
- Describe how your play putty feels.
- Tell how we made the play putty.
- Explain how you fly a kite.
- Compare play putty to Play-Doh.

Application
- What would be wrong with using a glue stick to make play putty?
- Name three toys you use inside and three toys you use outside.
- Tell about your favorite toy.
- Did you ever break a toy? Tell about it.

Analysis
- How are a drum and whistle the same?
- Tell how a teddy bear and a puppet are different.
- What is the opposite of *work*?
- You stack blocks. You fly a _____.

Synthesis
- Think of all the things you can do with play putty.
- Create a new toy and tell about it.
- What would it be like if you had no toys?
- What would happen if you were flying a kite and the string broke?

Evaluation
- Would you rather work a puzzle or play with a puppet? Why?
- Would you rather play inside or outside? Why?
- Would you rate your play putty as good or poor? Why?

Sports

Project

"Simon Says"

Simon says, "Hop on one foot."

Directions:
- Have the children stand in a line.
- Select one child to be Simon.
- Simon tells the children to do an action and those children act out the action. Possible actions/verbs include *jump, skip, throw, run, dribble, shoot, roll, swim, hop,* and *kick*.

Sports

Picture Cards

➡ **Objective**: The child will increase receptive understanding and expressive use of sports vocabulary.

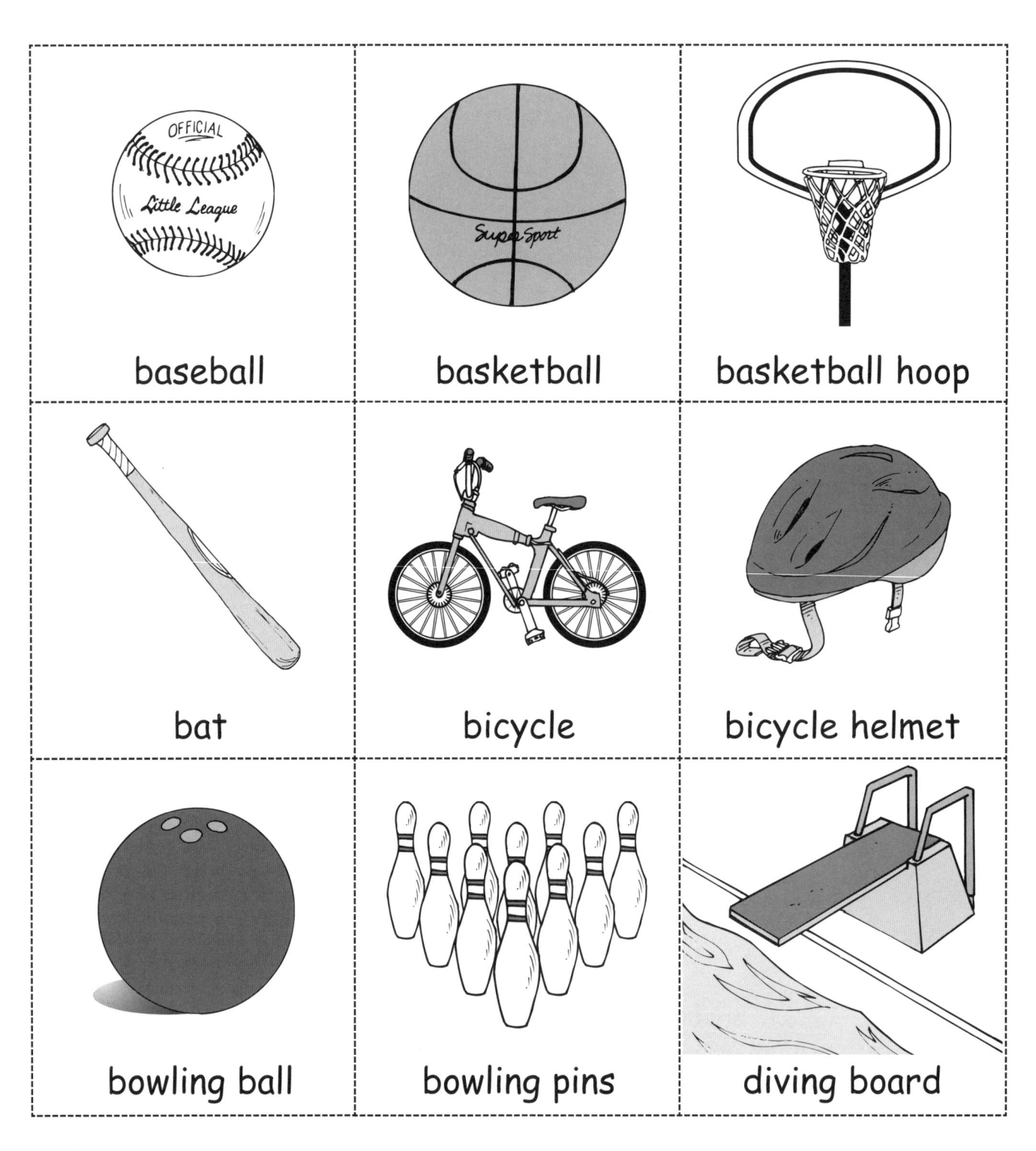

baseball	basketball	basketball hoop
bat	bicycle	bicycle helmet
bowling ball	bowling pins	diving board

Unit 10
Blooming Category Activities

Copyright © 2006 LinguiSystems, Inc.

Sports

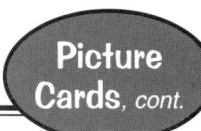

Picture Cards, *cont.*

football	golf ball	golf club
helmet	knee pads	roller blades
skateboard	skateboard ramp	ski poles

Sports

Picture Cards, cont.

snow skis	soccer ball	soccer net
swimming goggles	swimming pool	tennis ball
tennis racket	volleyball	volleyball net

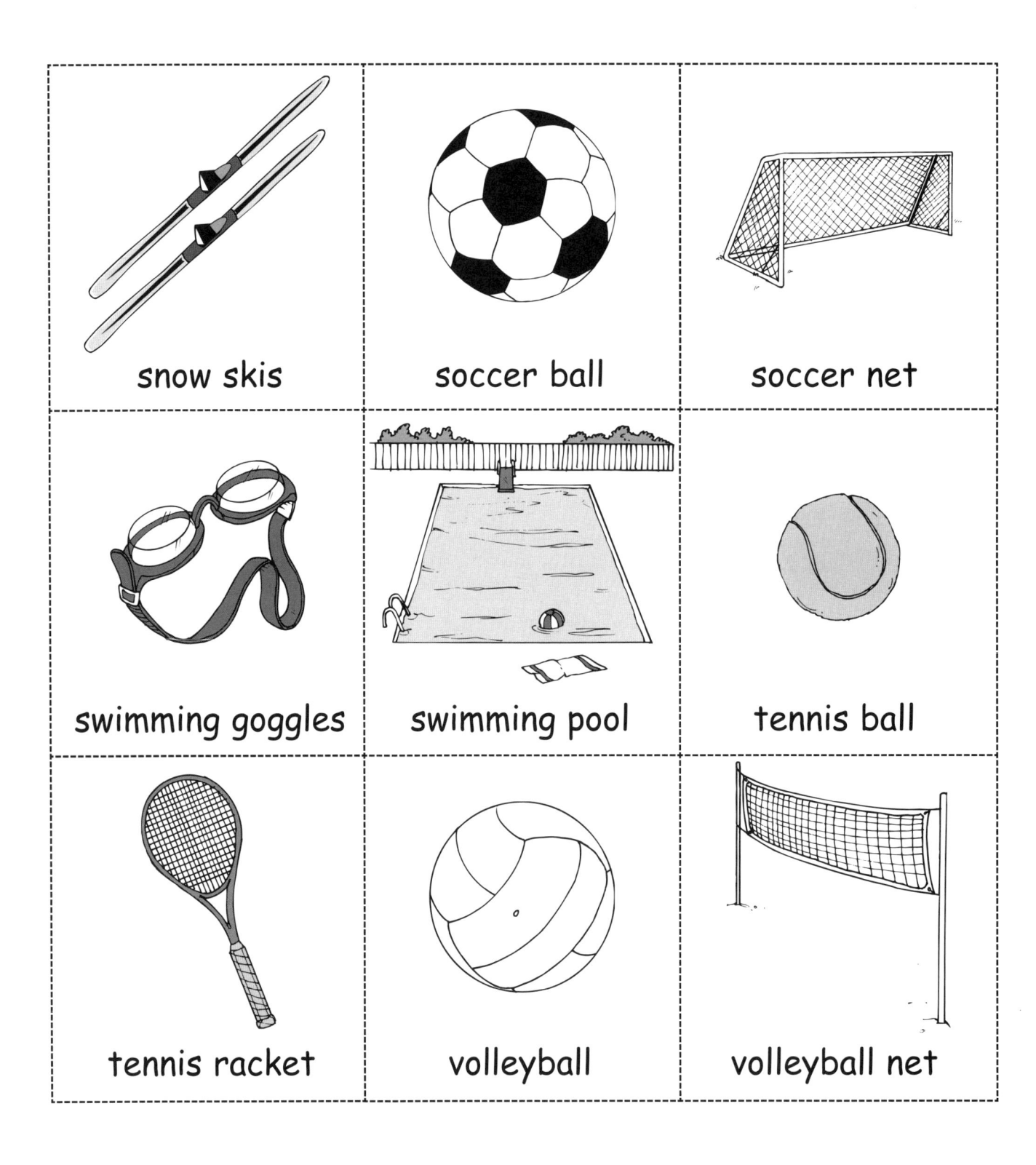

Unit 10
Blooming Category Activities

Sports

Family Letter

Dear Family,

In speech, we are learning about sports and the vocabulary that goes with this category. You can help your child practice this vocabulary at home. Talk about the picture below with your child and help him use sports words to answer the questions. Then put this page in a high traffic area in your home to remind everyone to help your child talk about sports. Some ideas to encourage this are listed at the bottom of the page.

Thank you, _____

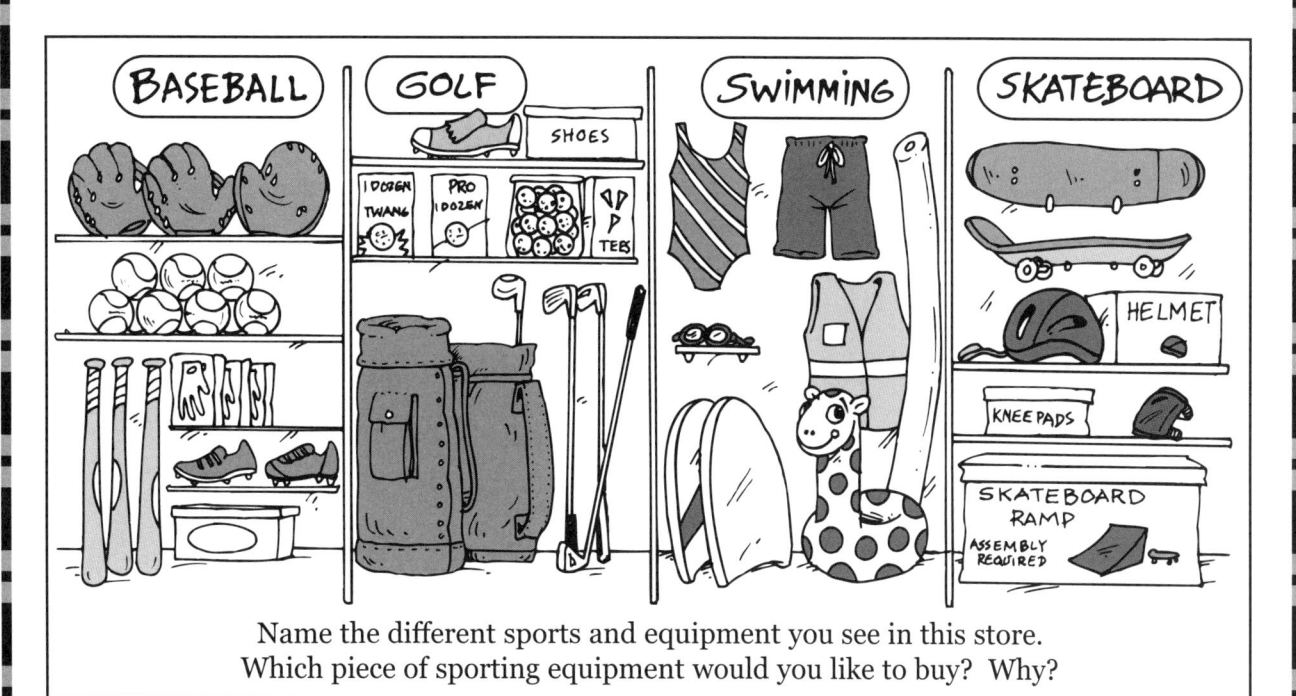

Name the different sports and equipment you see in this store.
Which piece of sporting equipment would you like to buy? Why?

- Mom likes to play **golf**.
- I play **soccer** with my friends.
- **Catch** the **ball** with two hands.
- **Football players** wear **helmets**.
- John scored a **touchdown** in the **football game**.

- **Volleyball** players are tall.
- Let's go **swimming**.
- We **ski** in the mountains.
- He made a **basket**.
- Put **knee** and **elbow pads** on before you **skateboard**.

Unit 10
Blooming Category Activities 111 Copyright © 2006 LinguiSystems, Inc.

Sports

Activities

For some of these activities, you will photocopy and cut apart the picture cards on pages 108-110.

- Sing "This is the Way" and use sports-related verb phrases, such as *kick the ball*, *hit the ball*, and *run the bases*.

- Put the pictures of the sports equipment in a bag. Have the child pull out a picture, name the item, and tell what sport it is used in.

- Use real sports balls and have the child sort them by size.

- Cut out pictures of different sports from magazines or newspapers. Put the pictures facedown in a pile. Have the child choose a card and then pretend to play that sport.

- Use a toy bowling set and bowl. Have the child count the number of pins he knocks down each time.

- Encourage turn-taking and group interaction while playing games such as "Duck, Duck, Goose" or "Ring Around the Rosie."

- Set up an obstacle course. As the child runs the course, have him tell what he is doing using concepts such as *throwing the ball over the stick*, *crawling under the chair*, and *putting the ball in the basket*.

- Use two sets of cards and play "Memory." Have the child name each picture he turns over. When he makes a match, have him say what he would do with that item.

- Put different balls in a box. Let the child pull out a ball, name it, and then describe it.

- Put a paper clip on each picture card. Make a fishing pole by tying some string to the end of a stick and then tying a magnet onto the other end of the string. Let the child "fish" for sports cards. Have him name each sports card he "catches" and tell an item related to it.

- Have the child draw a picture of or bring in a photograph of a sport he plays. Then have him tell about the sport.

- Sing "Take Me Out to the Ball Game" and talk about the sport of baseball.

- Place hula hoops on the floor and have the children throw bean bags into them. To make it a contest, assign different points to each hoop. The child with the most points wins. During play, encourage the children to use prepositional phrases, such as *in the hula hoop*, *on the skateboard*, and *next to the helmet*.

- Do a beanbag toss. Put picture cards on the floor. Have the child throw a beanbag and name the picture card the beanbag lands on.

Sports

Worksheet

➤ **Objective:** The child will increase his understanding of categories by choosing sports items that go together.

Have the child point to each target picture and say the word. Then have him name the other three pictures in the row. Tell him to circle the pictures that go with the target word and to put an X on each picture that doesn't go with it. Finally, have him tell why the pictures do or do not go with the target word.

1. mitt
2. golf club
3. bike
4. skis
5. hoop
6. football

Unit 10
Blooming Category Activities

Sports

Concepts

➡ **Objective**: The child will demonstrate receptive understanding and expressive use of basic concepts while completing the activity.

What's Missing?

Materials:
- a photocopy of the picture scene on page 115 for each child
- crayons, markers, or pencils

Directions:
- Give each child a picture scene and a marker, crayon, or pencil.
- Have one child look at the picture and tell one item that's missing.
- The child then draws in the missing item and tells where he drew it.

Suggested Concepts to Target:

- **over/under** — The boy kicked the ball **over** the net.
  The tail is **under** the kite.

- **left/right** — I draw with my **left** hand.
  The boy is kicking with his **right** leg.

- **on/off** — The boy is standing **on** the skateboard.
  The girl is getting **off** the bike.

- **first/last** — I drew the missing ball **first**.
  The **last** thing I drew was the skateboard.

- **before/after** — **Before** you can fly a kite, you need to add a tail.
  After you fly a kite, you have to wind up the string.

- **in front/behind** — The boy is **in front** of the skateboard ramp.
  Draw a ball **behind** the girl on the bike.

- **same/different** — I colored my kite the **same** as yours.
  Your tennis racquet looks **different** than mine.

- **near/far** — The dog is **near** the boy.
  The soccer net is **far** away from the basketball court.

Concepts, cont.

Sports

Unit 10
Blooming Category Activities

Sports

Bloom's Taxonomy

→ **Objective**: The child will answer increasingly more difficult questions about sports based on *Bloom's Taxonomy of Educational Objectives*.

Ask these questions while doing the "Simon Says" activity on page 107 and throughout all of the activities in this lesson.

Knowledge
- What do you use to hit a baseball?
- Name three actions we did during "Simon Says."
- Who can run faster, you or your mom?
- How many times did we jump?

Comprehension
- Describe a soccer ball.
- Define the word *sports*.
- Compare a baseball and golf ball.
- Tell how we played "Simon Says."

Application
- Tell about a sport you like to play.
- Name two sports with balls and two sports without balls.
- Tell two winter sports and two summer sports.
- Name other things we could do when playing "Simon Says."

Analysis
- Why do football players wear helmets?
- Finish this: You hit a baseball. You bounce a _____.
- What is the opposite of *run*?
- How is T-ball like baseball? How is it different?

Synthesis
- Create a new sport and tell how you would play it.
- Draw a picture of a new soccer uniform.
- If you wanted to be in the Olympics, which sport would you try out for? Why?
- Think of all the ways you can swim.

Evaluation
- What was your favorite thing we did in "Simon Says"? Why?
- What is your favorite sport? Why?
- What is your favorite sports team? Why?

School

Project

Packing a Backpack for School

Materials:
- backpack
- school supplies, such as *a glue stick, a ruler, a pen, pencils, paper, a folder, a workbook, a lunchbox, a box of crayons,* and *scissors*

Directions:
- Have the child pack her backpack for school. As the child puts each item in the bag, ask her to say its name and tell how she would use it. Also ask her when she would use it at school.
- Work on developing receptive vocabulary by telling the child which item to pack. Be certain to use concept words when you give directions, such as *Put the scissors in first, Put the pencil in next,* and *The glue stick should go in last.*

School

Picture Cards

Objective: The child will increase receptive understanding and expressive use of school vocabulary.

backpack	bookcase	calendar
chalk	chalkboard	computer
crayons	cubby	desk

Unit 11
Blooming Category Activities

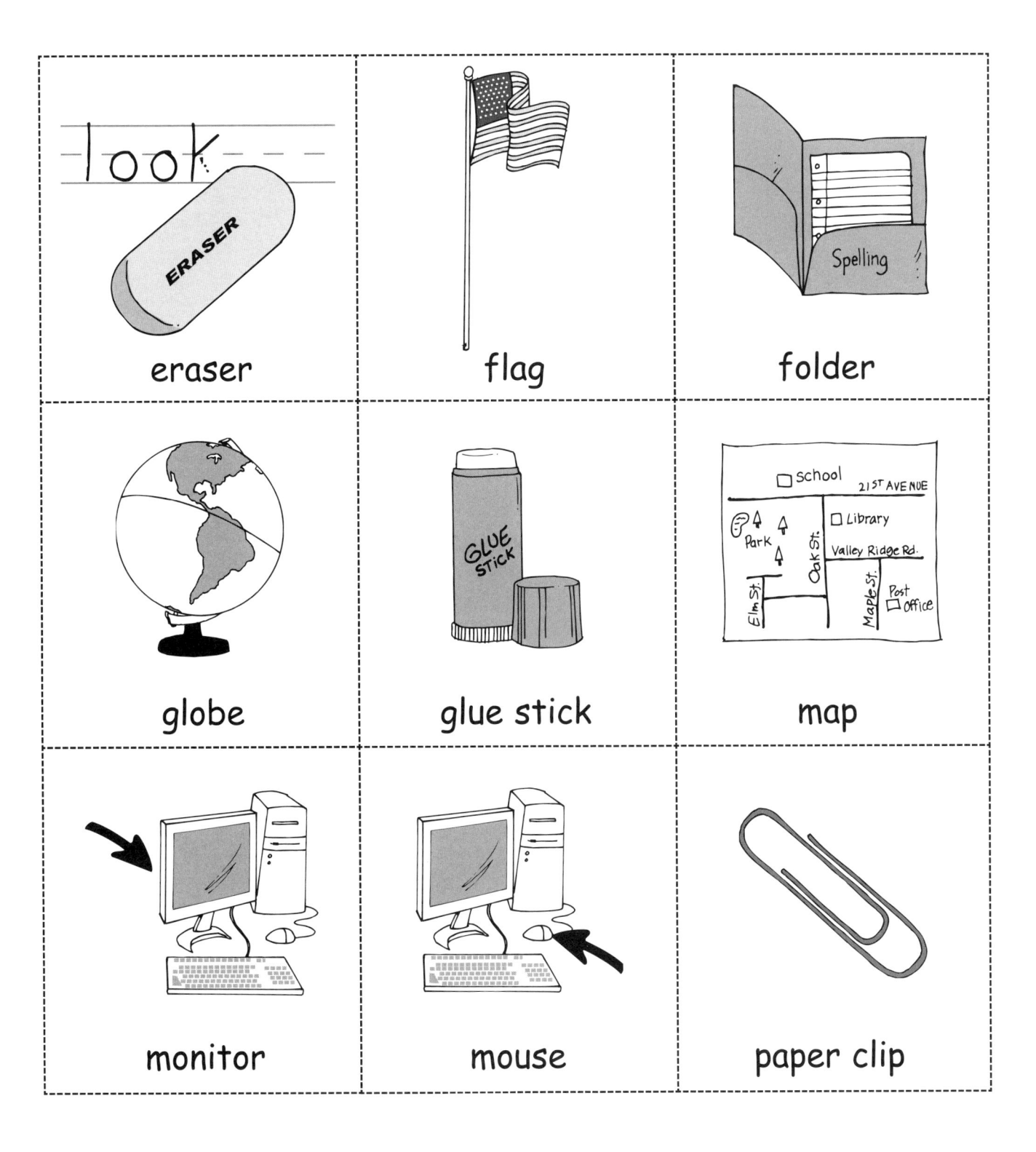

School

Picture Cards, *cont.*

eraser	flag	folder
globe	glue stick	map
monitor	mouse	paper clip

Unit 11
Blooming Category Activities

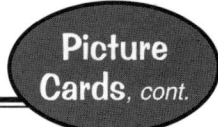

School

Picture Cards, cont.

pencil	pencil sharpener	ruler
school bus	scissors	student
teacher	workbook	yardstick

Unit 11
Blooming Category Activities

School

Family Letter

Dear Family,

In speech, we are learning about school and the vocabulary that goes with that category. You can help your child practice this vocabulary at home. Talk about the picture below with your child and help her use school words to answer the questions. Then put this page in a high traffic area in your home to remind everyone to help your child talk about school vocabulary. Some ideas to encourage this are listed at the bottom of the page.

Thank you, _____

These children are getting on the school bus. How do you go to school?

- My **homework** was in the **workbook**.
- Those **scissors** are sharp.
- My **teacher** is nice.
- Put your **paper** in your **backpack**.
- A new **student** came to our **class**.

- I used a **ruler** to draw a straight line.
- We found Asia on the **globe**.
- My **glue stick** is gone.
- We worked on the **computer**.
- I keep my **crayons** in my **desk**.

Unit 11
Blooming Category Activities

School

Activities

For some of these activities, you will photocopy and cut apart the picture cards on pages 118-120.

- Place a set of picture cards in a backpack. Have the child pull out a picture, name it, and tell how it is used in a classroom.

- Put the school supply pictures around the room. Then let the child go shopping for back-to-school supplies.

- Play school. Have the children sing songs like the " The Alphabet Song."

- Place the picture cards faceup on a table. Give a definition of an item. Then have the child select the item and tell its name.

- Have the child tell about her daily school activities. Be sure she uses the target vocabulary as she talks about her routine.

- Ask the child how she gets to school. Have her tell about the things she sees as she travels to school.

- Put all of the picture cards in a box. Have the child pull out a card and then act out how she would use the item. Let the other children guess the name of the item.

- Have the child say the alphabet. After each letter, have her tell the name of something at school that starts with that letter.

- Put the picture cards into a lunch box and have the child pull out two cards. Then have her use the two words in a sentence.

- Use a set of school picture cards and a set of picture cards from any other unit in this book. Mix the picture cards together and have the child choose one. Let her tell if the item is a school item or if it belongs to another category.

- Take pictures of activities that happen at school. Print the pictures, and have the child sequence them in the order that they occur during the school day. Have her tell a story about her school day. This is a good time to work on verb tenses. Make sure the child uses the correct verb tenses while telling her story.

School

Worksheet

➡ **Objective:** The child will be able to categorize items by location.

Directions:
- Make photocopies of this page and page 124 for each child.
- Have the child name the items on both pages.
- Have her cut out the pictures on this page and glue them in the correct column on page 124. (Some items may belong in more than one category.)
- Talk about how the items go together.

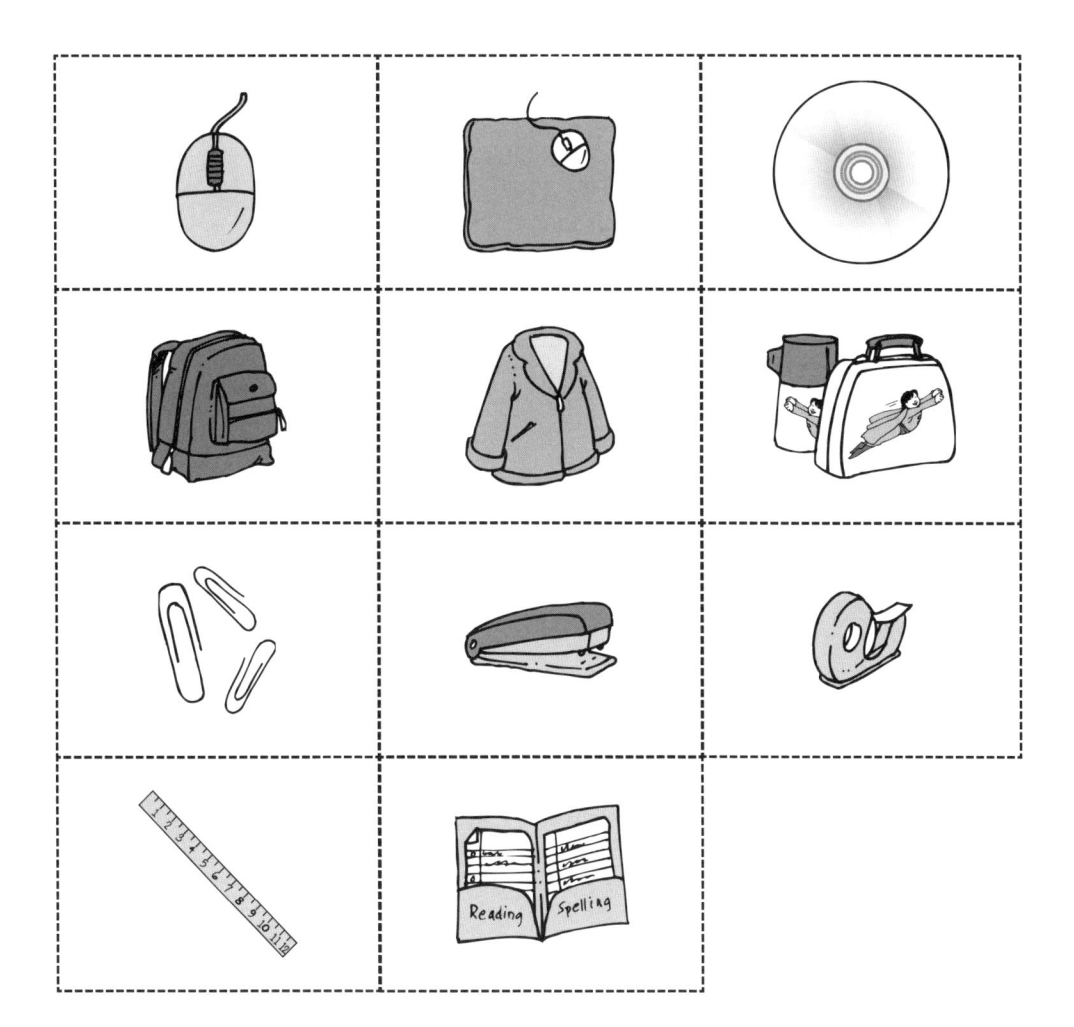

Unit 11
Blooming Category Activities

Copyright © 2006 LinguiSystems, Inc.

School

Worksheet, cont.

computer	lockers	desk

Unit 11
Blooming Category Activities

School

Concepts

➡ **Objective**: The child will demonstrate receptive understanding and expressive use of basic concepts while completing the activity.

Back to School

Materials:
- glue
- scissors
- photocopies of pages 126 and 127 for each child

Directions:
- Have the child name each item on page 126.
- Let her color the items and cut them out.
- Give the child directions for gluing the items onto the classroom scene on page 127, using prompts such as the ones listed below.
- After all the items are glued onto the scene, work on the child's expressive knowledge of the concepts by having her tell where each item is glued.

Suggested Concepts to Target:

- **left/right**
  Put the bookcase to the **left** of the chalkboard.
  Glue the globe on the **right** end of the bookcase.

- **next to/beside**
  Glue the calendar on the wall **next to** the chalkboard.
  Glue the yardstick **beside** the globe.

- **over/under/below**
  Glue the clock **over** a bookcase.
  Put the eraser **under** the chalkboard.
  Glue the map **below** the calendar.

- **between/center**
  Put the desk **between** two other desks.
  Glue the can of pencils in the **center** of the teacher's desk.

- **in the corner**
  Put the flag **in the corner** of the room.

- **on/off**
  Glue the pencil sharpener **on** the teacher's desk.
  Take the cap **off** of the glue stick.

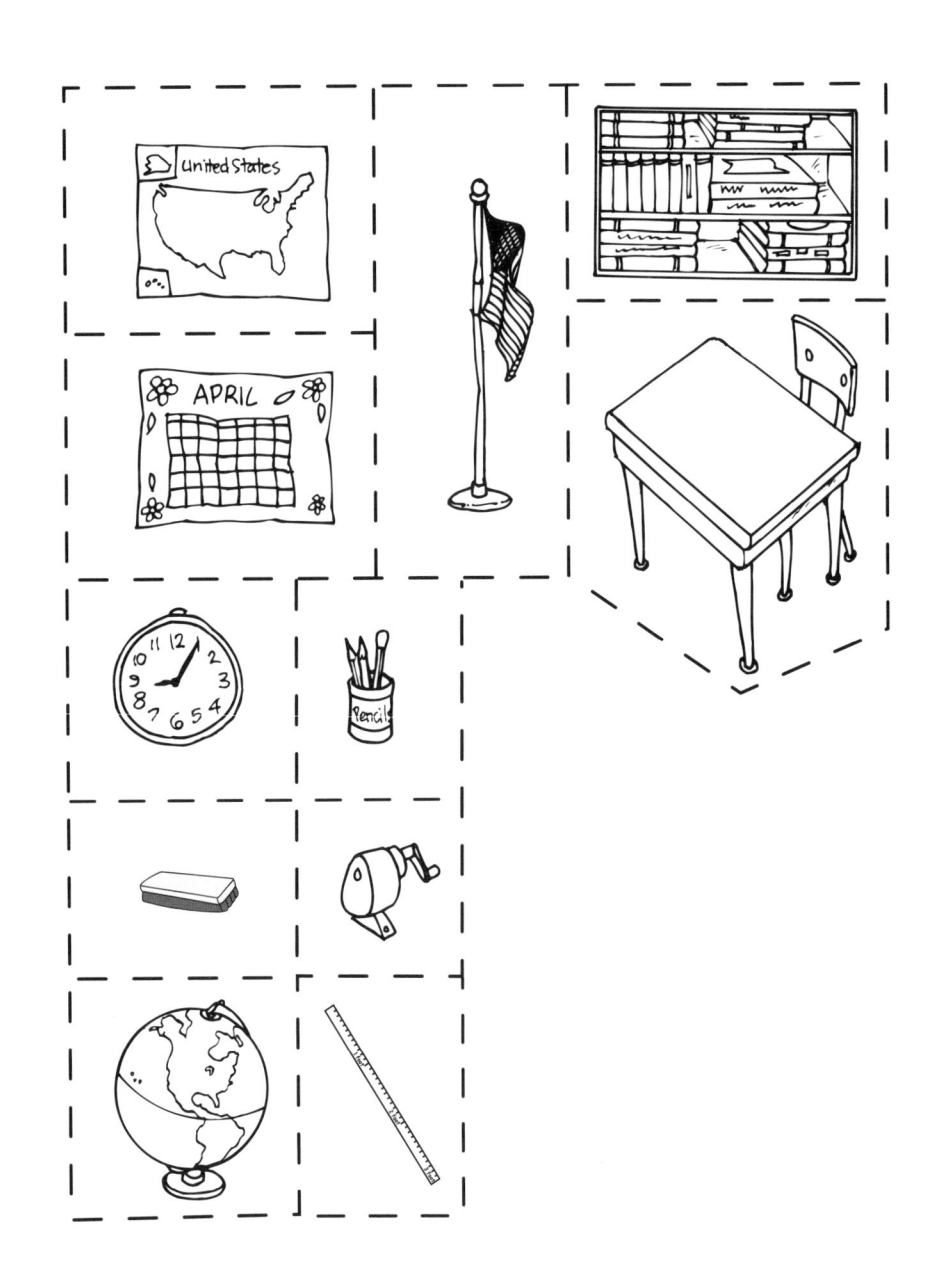

School

Concepts, *cont.*

Concepts, *cont.*

School

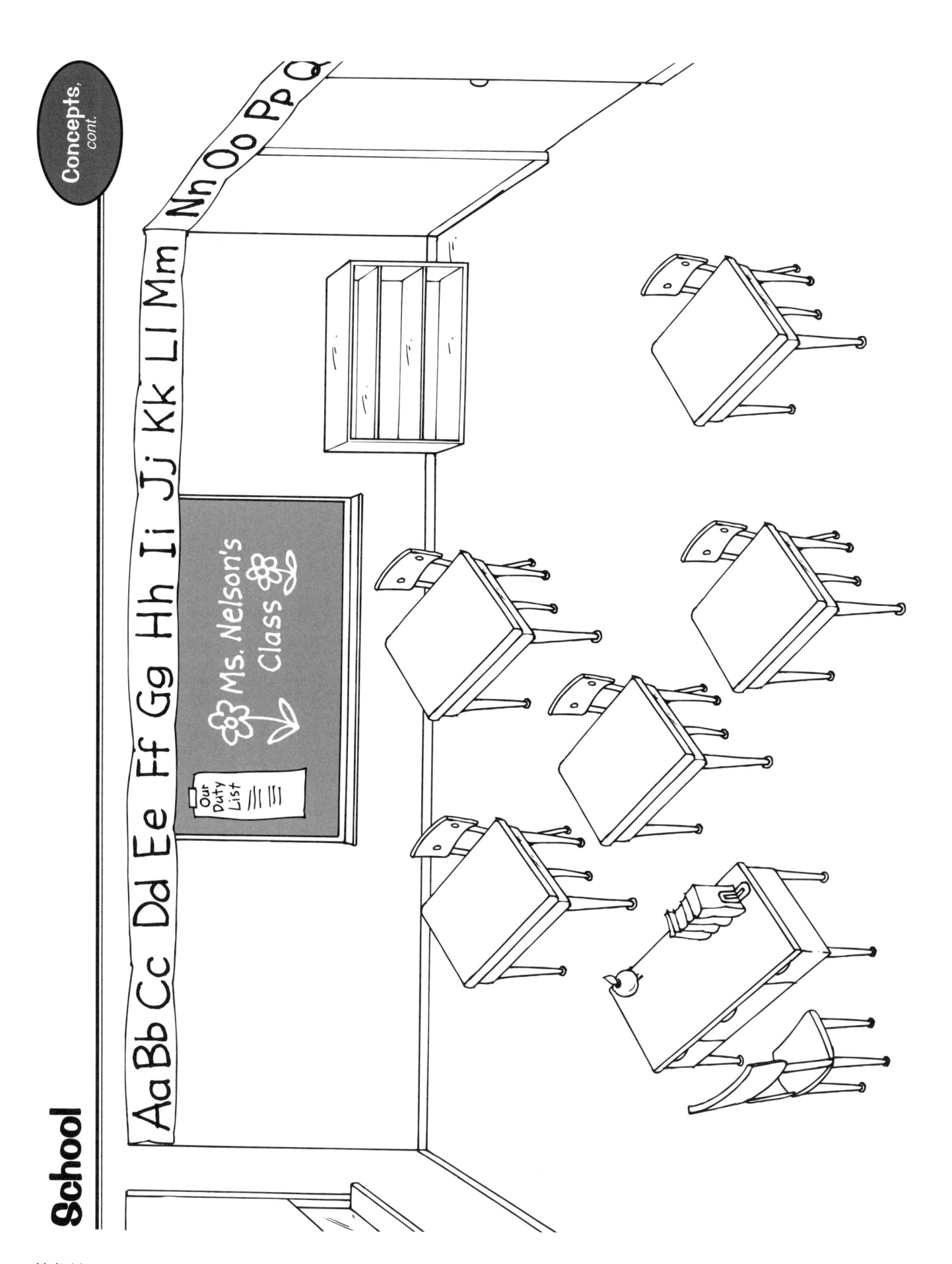

Aa Bb Cc Dd Ee Ff Gg Hh Ii Jj Kk Ll Mm Nn Oo Pp Qq

Ms. Nelson's Class

Our Duty List

Unit 11
Blooming Category Activities

127

Copyright © 2006 LinguiSystems, Inc.

School

Bloom's Taxonomy

Objective: The child will answer increasingly more difficult questions about school based on *Bloom's Taxonomy of Educational Objectives*.

Ask these questions while doing the Packing a Backpack for School activity on page 117 and throughout all of the activities in this lesson.

Knowledge
- How many things did we put in our backpack?
- Who is your best friend at school?
- Where do you put your backpack when you get to school?
- What is your teacher's name?

Comprehension
- Give an example of something you write with at school.
- Explain what you do with a globe.
- Describe how you use scissors.
- Draw a picture of your backpack and tell about it.

Application
- Name two things you write with and two things you write on.
- What else could we put in our backpack?
- What is wrong with putting ice cream in your lunch box?
- What is another word for *instructor*?

Analysis
- How are a yardstick and a ruler the same?
- How are a pen and a pencil different?
- What is the first thing you do when you get to school? What is the last thing you do before you leave school?
- Pen is to paper as chalk is to _____.

Synthesis
- Think of all the things you could use to color a picture.
- What would you do if you were the principal?
- What would it be like if you had to move to a new school?
- You studied hard for a test. How do you think you did?

Evaluation
- What is your favorite school subject? Why?
- Which would you rather write with, a pen or a computer? Why?
- Would you rather use a glue stick or a bottle of glue? Why?

Holidays

Project

Holiday Headband

Materials:
- holiday pictures on page 135
- markers or crayons
- long, narrow strips of construction paper
- stapler
- glue
- scissors

Directions:
- Make a photocopy of the holiday pictures on page 135 for each child.
- Have the child color and cut out the pictures.
- Cut a two-inch-wide strip of construction paper that is long enough to go around the child's head.
- Have the child choose a holiday picture, name it, and tell the holiday it is associated with.
- Let the child glue the picture to his headband.
- Staple the ends of the headband together so that it will fit on the child's head.

Holidays

Picture Cards

➡ **Objective:** The child will increase receptive understanding and expressive use of holiday vocabulary.

birthday	calendar	card
confetti	costume	crayon
decorate	fireworks	flag

Unit 12
Blooming Category Activities

Holidays

Picture Cards, cont.

flowers	Halloween	heart
holidays	Indian	Jack-o'-lantern
leprechaun	New Year's Day	noisemaker

Unit 12
Blooming Category Activities

Holidays

Picture Cards, *cont.*

parade	party hat	Pilgrim
shamrock	St. Patrick's Day	Thanksgiving
trick or treat	turkey	Valentine's Day

Holidays

Family Letter

Dear Family,

In speech, we are learning about holidays and the vocabulary that goes with that category. You can help your child practice this vocabulary at home. Talk about the picture below with your child and help him use holiday words to answer the questions. Then put this page in a high traffic area in your home or in the car to remind everyone to help your child talk about holidays. Some ideas to encourage this are listed at the bottom of the page.

Thank you, _____

What holiday is this? How does your family celebrate Independence Day?

- My **birthday** is next week.
- We watched the **fireworks** over the lake.
- Let's carve a **jack-o'-lantern**.
- Mom is making the **turkey**.
- We are going to Grandma's for **Thanksgiving**.

- Let's make breakfast for **Mother's Day**.
- I wore a **costume** for **Halloween**.
- I gave my friend a **valentine**.
- Remember to wear green on **St. Patrick's Day**.
- Can we stay up until midnight on **New Year's Eve**?

Unit 12
Blooming Category Activities

Holidays

Activities

For some of these activities, you will photocopy and cut apart the picture cards on pages 130-132.

- Let the child make a greeting card for a holiday. As he decorates the card, have him use target vocabulary words to talk about the holiday.

- Put the picture cards into a bag. Have the child pull out a card, say the name of the picture, and tell what holiday it is associated with. Sort the picture cards by holiday.

- Let the child decorate and eat a holiday cookie. As he decorates, have him talk about what he is doing. Encourage him to use verbs, such as *sprinkle, spread, taste,* and *eat.*

- Have the child draw a holiday picture. As he draws the picture, encourage him to use holiday vocabulary and talk about his holiday experiences.

- Make a peanut butter and jelly sandwich. When you are done, use a cookie cutter to cut it into a holiday shape.

- Cut out different-sized shapes, such as *hearts, pumpkins, turkeys,* and *shamrocks.* Have the child sort the shapes by size or by holiday. Use comparatives and superlatives, such as *big, bigger,* and *biggest,* to describe the shapes.

- Play a "hopping" game, such as *heart hop, shamrock shuffle,* or *turkey trot.* Use holiday shapes to make a path on the floor. Then have the child hop from one shape to another after he names an item that goes with the holiday.

- Read a book about a holiday. After each page, ask the child questions that he can answer using correct syntax.

- Cut out leaves or turkey feathers from different-colored sheets of construction paper. Have the child choose a leaf or feather and name the color.

- Use a brown paper grocery bag to make a vest. Have the child decorate his vest with different holiday shapes. Be sure the child tells you the name of the shape and which holiday it is associated with.

- Have the child plan a holiday party. Let him decide what foods he would have and which games he would play.

- Make a mask from a paper plate. Cut out two holes in the plate for the eyes. Have the child decorate the plate using fun decorations like buttons, glitter, and yarn. Punch a hole on each side of the plate and tie a piece of string (12 – 16 inches long) on each side. Hold the mask up to the child's face and tie the two pieces of yarn together behind his head to secure the mask.

Holidays

Worksheet

Objective: The child will demonstrate receptive understanding and expressive use of temporal concepts related to holidays.

Directions:
- Make photocopies of the calendar on page 136 and the holiday pictures on this page for each child.
- Cut out the holiday pictures.
- Have the child select one holiday picture, name the item, and tell what holiday it is associated with.
- Let the child tell what month the holiday is in and find that month on the calendar. (Some months may have two pictures.)
- Have him glue the picture to the calendar.
- Encourage use of temporal concepts, such as *first*, *last*, *before*, and *after*.

Unit 12
Blooming Category Activities

Holidays

Worksheet, *cont.*

JANUARY	MAY	SEPTEMBER
FEBRUARY	JUNE	OCTOBER
MARCH	JULY	NOVEMBER
APRIL	AUGUST	DECEMBER

Holidays

Concepts

➤ **Objective**: The child will demonstrate receptive understanding and expressive use of basic concepts while completing the activity.

Jack-O'-Lantern

Materials:
- one sheet of orange construction paper or a small real pumpkin for each child
- markers

Directions:
- If you're using construction paper, draw a pumpkin outline on the sheet.
- Tell the child to follow your instructions and draw facial features on the pumpkin. Be sure to use concepts in your directions.

Suggested Concepts to Target:

- **left/right**
  Make the **left** eye a circle.
  Draw a triangle for the **right** eye.

- **same/different**
  Make the pumpkin's ears the **same** shape.
  My pumpkin looks **different** than yours looks.

- **over/under**
  The eyes are **over** the nose.
  Draw a mouth **under** the nose.

- **between/next to**
  The nose is **between** the eyes.
  Draw some hair **next to** the pumpkin's stem.

- **first/middle/last**
  I drew the nose **first**.
  I put the mouth in the **middle** of the pumpkin.
  I drew the pumpkin's ears **last**.

- **top/middle/bottom**
  The stem is on the **top**.
  Draw the nose in the **middle** of the pumpkin.
  Put the mouth on the **bottom** of the face.

- **before/after**
  Draw the eyes **before** you draw the mouth.
  After you draw the mouth, draw the nose.

Holidays

Bloom's Taxonomy

Objective: The child will answer increasingly more difficult questions about holidays based on *Bloom's Taxonomy of Educational Objectives.*

Ask these questions while doing the Holiday Headband activity on page 129 and throughout all of the activities in this lesson.

Knowledge
- When do we see fireworks?
- What holiday shapes did you put on your headband?
- How many shapes are on your headband?
- Who helped you make your headband?

Comprehension
- Explain how you made your headband.
- Describe Valentine's Day.
- Give an example of Thanksgiving food.
- Where do pumpkins grow?

Application
- Name some other shapes you can put on your headband.
- What would be wrong with celebrating New Year's Day in the summer?
- What is another name for *Independence Day*?
- Tell how your family celebrates Valentine's Day.

Analysis
- How are Halloween and Thanksgiving alike?
- Compare your headband to your friend's.
- What are the steps we used to make your headband?
- A heart is to Valentine's Day as a shamrock is to _____.

Synthesis
- Create a song to celebrate New Year's Day.
- How else could you fasten your headband?
- What would it be like if we did not have a calendar?
- How could we make our headbands better?

Evaluation
- Which holiday is your favorite? Why?
- Which holiday do you like decorating for better, Halloween or Independence Day? Why?
- Which is your favorite Thanksgiving food? Why?

Plants and Trees

Project

Leaf Rubbings

Materials:
- a sheet of white paper for each child
- crayons
- a variety of kinds and sizes of leaves (artificial leaves will work if real leaves are not available)

Directions:
- Look at and describe all of the leaves, using size, shape, color, and texture adjectives.
- Choose a leaf and put it under a sheet of paper.
- Use a crayon to color on top of the paper, over the leaf.
- The outline and the details of the leaf will appear on the paper.
- You can make several different leaf rubbings on one page.
- Discuss what kinds of trees the leaves come from.
- Talk about how some leaves appear in the spring and fall off in the autumn or die out in the winter.
- Talk about leaves we can eat, such as *lettuce*, *spinach*, and *cabbage*.

Plants and Trees

Picture Cards

➡ **Objective:** The child will increase receptive understanding and expressive use of vocabulary related to plants and trees.

branch	bud	bulbs
bush	cactus	cones
dig	farm	fern

Unit 13
Blooming Category Activities

Plants and Trees

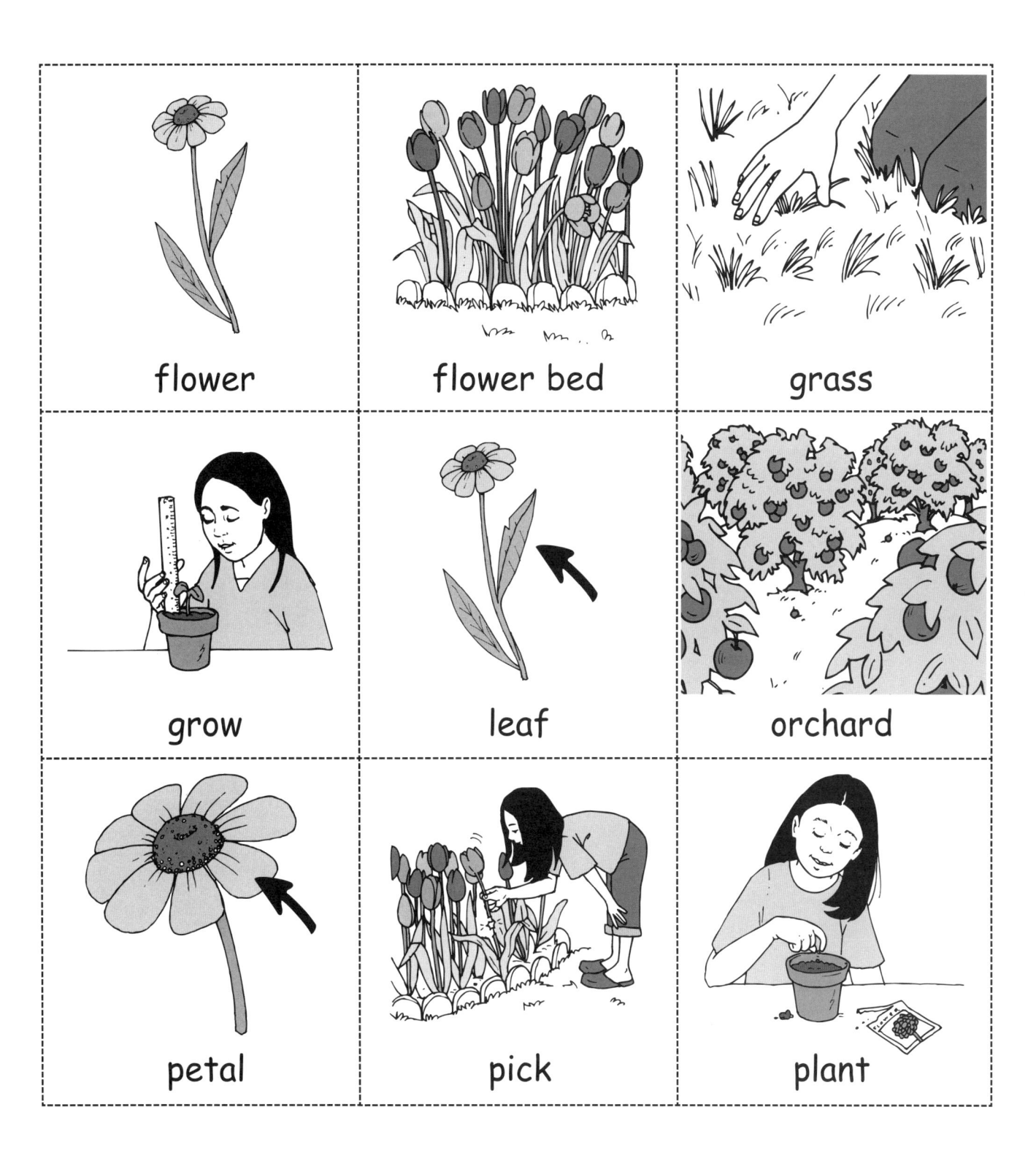

Picture Cards, *cont.*

flower	flower bed	grass
grow	leaf	orchard
petal	pick	plant

Unit 13
Blooming Category Activities

Plants and Trees

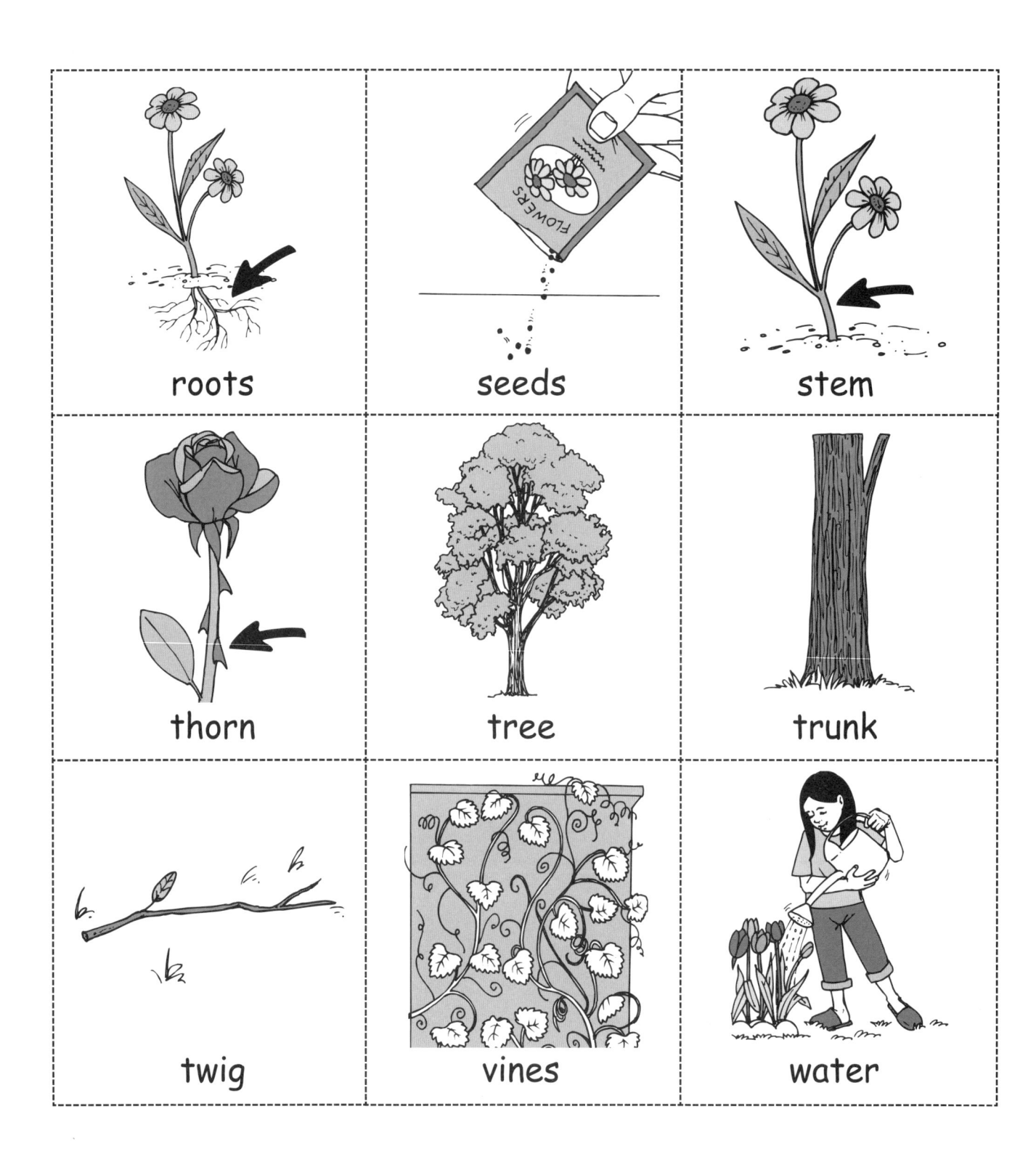

Picture Cards, cont.

roots	seeds	stem
thorn	tree	trunk
twig	vines	water

Unit 13
Blooming Category Activities

Plants and Trees

Family Letter

Dear Family,

In speech, we are learning about things that grow, such as plants and trees. You can help your child practice this vocabulary at home. Talk about the picture below with your child. Then put this page somewhere in your home to remind everyone to talk about plants, trees, and flowers. Perhaps you can take a nature hike in your yard or a nearby park and talk about all of the growing things that you see. Some other suggestions to encourage use of this vocabulary are included at the bottom of this page.

Thank you, _____

Name some vegetables that this family is growing in their garden. What kind of food would you like to grow?

- Dad is **mowing** the **grass**.
- Let's **plant** some **tomato plants**.
- I gave Mom a **bouquet** of **roses**.
- Please **water** the **garden**.
- We **planted bulbs** under the **ground**.

- These **seeds** are tiny.
- That bird built a nest in our **tree**.
- These **flowers** smell good.
- The **vine** is climbing the **tree trunk**.
- There are a lot of **trees** in the park.

Plants and Trees

Activities

For some of these activities, you will photocopy and cut apart the picture cards on pages 140-142.

- Select the picture cards that show parts of a flower and parts of a tree. Let the child draw a picture of a flower on one sheet of paper and a picture of a tree on another sheet. Have the child choose a picture card and name it. Then have her categorize it by placing it on the correct sheet of paper.

- Have the children plant seeds using Styrofoam cups, planting soil, large seeds, and water. Talk about the materials you use and the steps you take to plant the seeds. Discuss the best place to put the cup so that the seeds will grow.

- Pretend to grow from a tiny seed to a flower, or from a sapling to a big tree. Start out crouched on the floor. Talk about roots, stems, and trunks, and their need for sunlight and water for growth.

- Make flowers from pipe cleaners and squares of colored tissue paper. Be sure to describe the materials you use.

- Using books or pictures, talk about the different animals that make their homes in trees, such as *birds*, *monkeys*, and *squirrels*.

- Talk about trees and how they change during the four seasons. It should be easy to find picture books to illustrate this pattern/sequence. Use the concepts of *same* and *different* to discuss the trees in each season.

- Draw a tree on a large sheet of butcher paper or on the board. Pretend the picture cards are apples or leaves and tape them to the tree. Let the children take turns "picking" an apple or leaf and naming the picture card.

- Use real objects or pictures to compare seeds, acorns, and bulbs by size, shape, color, and texture. Talk about what kind of tree or plant might grow from each.

- While looking at a tree in the school yard or at a picture of a tree, talk about all of the ways that trees help the environment. For instance, they are homes for animals; they give us fruit and nuts to eat; and we use their wood to build homes, make paper, and burn in fires.

- Go on a nature hike in a park or on the playground and talk about all of the growing things that you see. Then go back to the room and choose all of the picture cards that you saw on your hike.

- Have the child draw a picture of a tree or a plant at home and tell about its parts, its size and color, and its location.

- Make two copies of the picture cards and play "Memory." Have the child name the picture pairs and use the target words in a sentence.

Plants and Trees

Worksheet

Objective: The child will increase receptive understanding and expressive use of vocabulary related to plants and trees and foods that grow on them.

Directions:
- Make photocopies of this page and page 146 for each child.
- Have the child cut out the pictures of food on this page.
- Once the child can name all the foods, discuss which foods grow on trees, on plants, on vines, and under the ground as roots.
- Have the children glue the food pictures onto the appropriate plants shown in the picture scene.

Unit 13
Blooming Category Activities
Copyright © 2006 LinguiSystems, Inc.

Worksheet, *cont.*

Plants and Trees

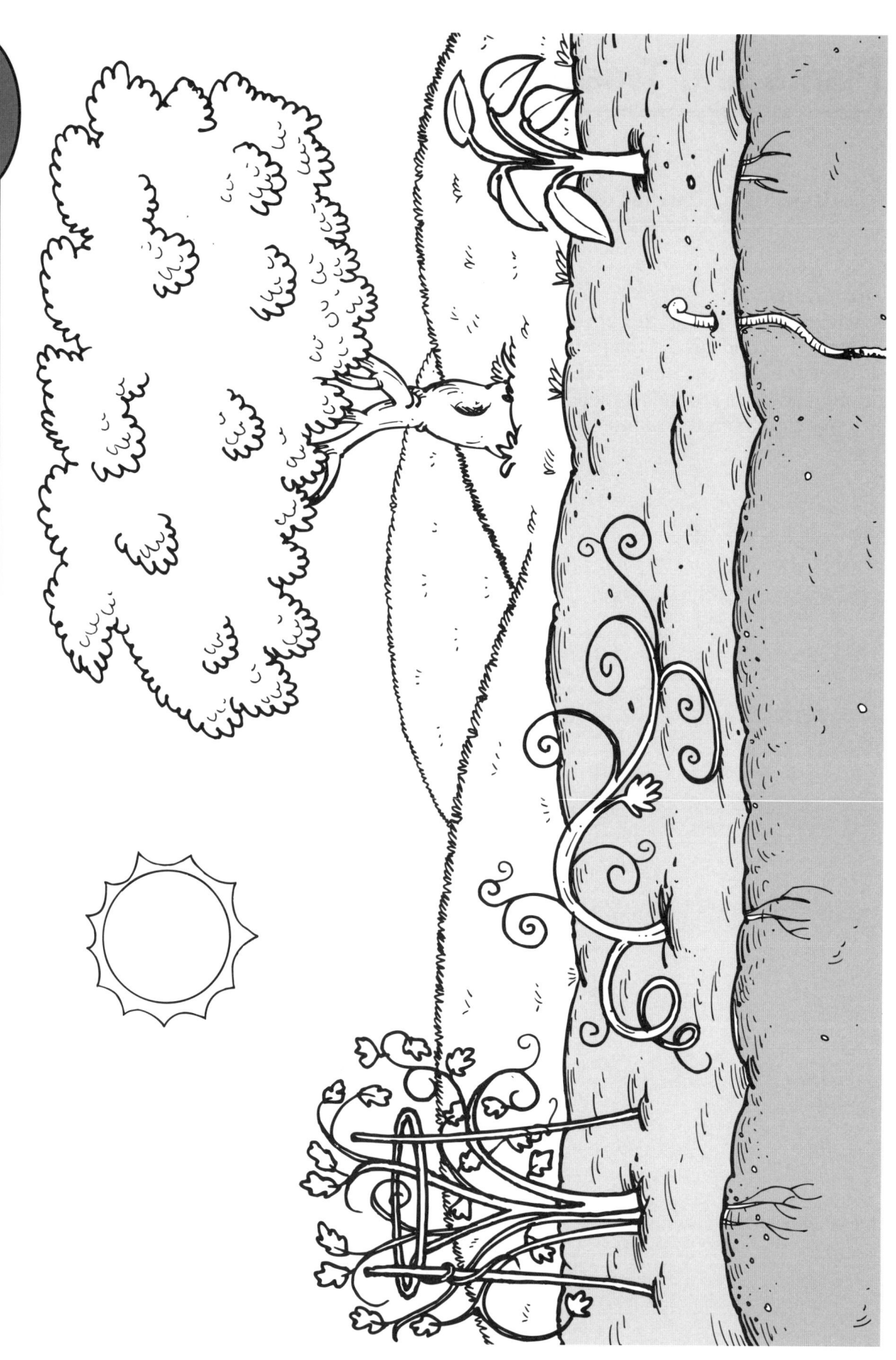

Unit 13
Blooming Category Activities — 146 — Copyright © 2006 LinguiSystems, Inc.

Plants and Trees

Concepts

→ **Objective**: The child will demonstrate receptive understanding and expressive use of basic concepts while completing the activity.

Making a Flower Garden

Materials:
- a photocopy of page 148 for each child
- crayons or markers
- scissors
- five wooden craft sticks or tongue depressors for each child
- glue or tape
- Styrofoam

Directions:
- Name all of the flowers on page 148. Then color them and cut them out.
- Glue or tape a flower to one end of each stick.
- "Plant" your garden by pushing the other end of each stick into the Styrofoam "flower bed."
- Compare the flowers by size, shape, and color and by which ones are your favorites.
- Use concept words to talk about where you planted each flower.

Suggested Concepts to Target:

- **in/on**
  Plant the lily **in** the garden.
  Glue the tulip **on** the stick.

- **left/right**
  The daisy is on the **left**.
  Put the rose on the **right** side of the tulip.

- **before/after**
  What did you do **before** you cut out the flowers?
  After you cut out the sunflower, glue it on the stick.

- **top/bottom**
  Glue the flower on the **top** of the stick.
  Push the **bottom** of the stick into the Styrofoam.

- **small/medium/big**
  The petals on the daisy are **small**.
  Put a **medium**-sized flower in next.
  The sunflower is **big**.

- **whole/part**
  We have finished the **whole** garden.
  What **part** of this craft do you like best?

- **beside/between**
  Which flower is **beside** the daisy?
  Put the rose **between** the sunflower and the tulip.

- **near/away from**
  I planted the rose **near** the tulip.
  The lily is **away from** the daisy.

Plants and Trees

Concepts, *cont.*

sunflower

rose

daisy

lily

tulip

Unit 13
Blooming Category Activities

Plants and Trees

Bloom's Taxonomy

➡ **Objective**: The child will answer increasingly more difficult questions about plants and trees based on *Bloom's Taxonomy of Educational Objectives*.

Ask these questions while doing the Leaf Rubbings activity on page 139 and throughout all of the activities in this lesson.

Knowledge
- What did you use to make the leaf picture?
- How many leaf rubbings did you make?
- Where can you find real leaves?
- Name two things that plants need to grow.

Comprehension
- Tell how you made the leaf rubbings.
- Match a leaf rubbing on your page with one on your friend's page.
- Describe your leaf picture.
- Draw a picture of a tree and name its parts.

Application
- Name two plants you can eat and two plants you can't eat.
- Name some other things we could make rubbings of.
- Tell about something you have planted.
- What's another word for *irrigate*?

Analysis
- How are some trees the same all year and how are some different?
- A flower has a stem and a tree has a _____.
- What could cause a plant to die?
- What steps should you follow to grow a tomato plant?

Synthesis
- Think of all the ways a farmer could water his crops.
- Create a new kind of tree and tell about it.
- How could we make our leaf picture better?
- Suppose you were a farmer. What kinds of crops would you grow?

Evaluation
- Which of your leaf pictures do you like best? Why?
- Would you rather be an oak tree or a rosebush? Why?
- Would you prefer to grow vegetables, sell them, or eat them? Tell why.

Ocean and Beach

Project

Making a Seashore Sandwich

Materials:
- one piece of bread
- grape jelly
- peanut butter
- fruit snack strips (about one inch long)
- goldfish-shaped crackers
- teddy bear-shaped cracker
- knife
- paper plate

Directions:
- Give each child a slice of bread, and have him put it on the paper plate.
- Let the child spread peanut butter on the top half of the bread. Talk about this being the "beach."
- Have him spread jelly on the bottom half of the bread. Explain that this is the "water."
- Let the child place some goldfish-shaped crackers on the jelly so the "fish are swimming in the water." Have him count the fish as he puts them on the jelly.
- Have him put the fruit snack strip on the peanut butter. Explain that this is the bear's beach towel.
- Have him place a teddy bear-shaped cookie on the fruit strip. The teddy bear is lying on the beach towel.

As you do this activity, be certain to use concept words when you give directions, such as "*Put the jelly on the **bottom** of the bread*," "*Put the bear **on** the fruit strip*," and "*The goldfish are **in** the water.*"

Also talk about the things you would see and use on a trip to the beach. For example, you might say, "The sand is near the water" or "You need a towel when you go to the beach."

Ocean and Beach

Picture Cards

Objective: The child will increase receptive understanding and expressive use of ocean and beach vocabulary.

beach towel	beach ball	build
deep	dig	flip-flops
float	kick	kickboard

Unit 14
Blooming Category Activities

151

Copyright © 2006 LinguiSystems, Inc.

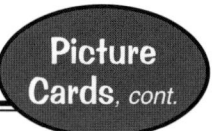

Ocean and Beach

Picture Cards, *cont.*

ocean	pail	sail
sandcastle	seahorse	seashells
seaweed	shallow	shovel

Unit 14
Blooming Category Activities

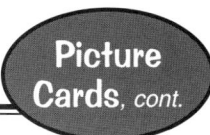

Ocean and Beach

Picture Cards, cont.

snorkel	splash	starfish
sun	sunglasses	sunscreen
surf	swim	wave

Unit 14
Blooming Category Activities

Ocean and Beach

Family Letter

Dear Family,

In speech, we are learning about the beach and ocean and the vocabulary that goes with this category. You can help your child practice this vocabulary at home. Talk about the picture below with your child and help him use the target words. Then put this page on your refrigerator or in another high traffic area to remind everyone to help your child talk about the beach and ocean. Some ideas to encourage this practice are listed at the bottom of the page. Thank you, _____

Where is this family? What are they doing at the beach?

- Take the **pail** and **shovel** with you.
- We built a large **sandcastle**.
- We can **swim** in the **ocean**.
- I found a **starfish**.
- Mom put the **seashells** in a jar.
- Matt knows how to **snorkel**.
- I felt **seaweed** in the **shallow** water.
- Put **sunscreen** on when you go outside.
- Mom likes to sit in a **beach chair** and read a book.
- The boy used a **kickboard** to help him **float**.

Ocean and Beach

Activities

For some of these activities, you will photocopy and cut apart the picture cards on pages 151-153.

- Bring in a beach bag and beach items, such as *a towel, sunglasses, sunscreen, flip flops, a shovel, and a pail*. Have the child put the items into the beach bag. Let him tell the name of each item and what he would use it for.

- Put sand into a large container. Bury the picture cards in the sand. Have the child use a shovel to dig out the pictures and name each picture he finds.

- Put the verb pictures in a pile. Have the child choose a picture and act out the verb.

- Have the child select five picture cards. Then have him draw a beach scene including the five pictures he chose.

- Bring in a container of sand and a pail of water. Pour the water on the sand. Let the child play in the sand and build a sandcastle. As he plays, have him talk about what he is doing.

- Use the picture cards to play "Go Fish." Have the child tell about each picture after he "catches" it.

- Fill a shoebox with beach items, such as *seashells, marine life pictures*, and *beach toys*. Have the child pull an item out of the box without looking at it. Have him feel the item and use shape, size, and texture adjectives to describe it.

- Let the child create a beach scene from pictures cut out of a magazine. Have the child talk about each picture, and, if appropriate, tell what he would do with the item. Let the child tell where he placed the picture, using concepts such as *above, below, next to*, and *in the corner*.

- Have two children roll a beach ball back and forth to each other. Have each child name a beach or ocean item as he rolls the ball to his friend.

- Make footprints and/or seashell shapes out of construction paper. Lay them on the floor to make a trail. The child will move from shape to shape by naming beach or ocean items. Each time he names a correct item, he can move forward to the next shape.

- Draw a line across the middle of a large sheet of construction paper, creating water and sand. Have the child select a picture card, tell its name, and then say if he would use it in the sand or in the water. Then let him glue it on the appropriate half of the construction paper.

Ocean and Beach

Worksheet

Objective: The child will demonstrate receptive understanding and expressive use of basic concepts.

Directions:
- Copy and cut apart a set of the picture cards below for each child.
- Give each child a copy of the picture scene on page 157, and place a set of picture cards facedown in front of him.
- Have the child draw a card, name the item, and tell if it belongs in the ocean or on the beach.
- Tell the child where to glue the picture on his beach scene. Your gluing directions should include concept words, such as *Glue the toy boat **on** the water* or *Glue the sunscreen **next to** the beach chair*.
- After the child glues the picture, have him tell where he glued it, using a concept word. For example, he might say, "The starfish is **next to** the seaweed" or "The towel is **on** the beach chair."

Ocean and Beach

Worksheet, *cont.*

Unit 14
Blooming Category Activities — 157 — Copyright © 2006 LinguiSystems, Inc.

Ocean and Beach

Concepts

➤ **Objective**: The child will demonstrate receptive understanding and expressive use of basic concepts while completing the activity.

Fish Jar

Materials:
- small, clean baby food jar with a lid and no label
- water
- blue food coloring
- fish-shaped stickers
- silver glitter

Directions:
- Let the child fill the baby food jar with water.
- Have him add several drops of blue food coloring and some glitter to the water.
- Put on the lid and close it tightly.
- Have the child put fish stickers on the outside of the jar. Tell him where to put the stickers by giving directions containing concept words, such as "Stick the yellow fish **above** the blue fish" and "Put the little fish **under** the big fish."
- Let the child shake the jar and watch the fish "swim."

Suggested Concepts to Target:

- **in/on**
  Put the blue food coloring **in** the water.
  Put the lid **on** the jar.

- **top/middle/bottom**
  The lid is on **top** of the jar.
  I put fish on the **middle** of the jar.
  The **bottom** of the jar is wet.

- **beside/next to**
  Put a red fish **beside** a blue fish.
  My fish jar is **next to** my friend's.

- **same/different**
  The yellow fish stickers look the **same**.
  Our fish jars look **different**.

- **before/after**
  I poured water in the jar **before** I added food coloring.
  After he finished the fish jar, he gave it to his mother.

- **first/last**
  The **first** thing he did was open the jar.
  He put the lid on the jar **last**.

- **few/more/most**
  She put a **few** drops of food coloring in the water.
  I have **more** fish on my jar than she does.
  His fish jar has the **most** glitter in it.

Ocean and Beach

Bloom's Taxonomy

Objective: The child will answer increasingly more difficult questions about ocean and beach based on *Bloom's Taxonomy of Educational Objectives*.

Ask these questions while doing the Making a Seashore Sandwich activity on page 150 and throughout all the activities in this lesson.

Knowledge
- Where did you put the teddy bear-shaped crackers?
- How many goldfish crackers did you use?
- What did you use to make sand?
- Name the things we used to create the beach scene.

Comprehension
- Draw a picture of a day at the beach.
- Describe how we made the seashore sandwich.
- Explain why we used a fruit strip for a beach towel.
- Compare smooth peanut butter to crunchy peanut butter.

Application
- Name some other things we could use for our beach scene.
- What else could you use to make water for our sandwich?
- Did you ever go to the beach and forget to bring a towel?
- What is another word for *swimsuit*?

Analysis
- What did you do first? What did you do last?
- How are sand and dirt the same?
- How are swimming and floating different?
- In the winter, I like to drink hot chocolate. In the summer, I like to _____.

Synthesis
- Create a way to make a seashore sandwich.
- What would it be like if you went swimming outdoors in the winter?
- Design a beach towel.
- Think of all the ways you could play at the beach or in the ocean.

Evaluation
- Do you like an ocean or a lake better for swimming? Why?
- Would it work to use a graham cracker instead of bread to make a seashore sandwich? Why?
- Could a real fish live in your fish jar? Why?

Musical Instruments

Project

Water Glass Xylophone

Materials:
- glass drinking glasses (number is optional)
- water
- metal spoon
- food coloring (optional)

Directions:
- Put the glasses in a row on the table.
- Put water in each glass, starting with a small amount in the first glass. Increase the amount of water in each glass in the row, so that the last glass is the fullest.
- (Optional) Put different colors of food coloring in each glass. Some can be mixed to make new colors.
- Using a metal spoon, tap the glasses and listen for the different tones.
- Take turns playing the musical xylophone.
- Talk about different musical instruments and encourage use of adjectives such as *high*, *low*, *slow*, *fast*, *soft*, *loud*, *first* and *last*.

Musical Instruments

Picture Cards

⇨ **Objective**: The child will increase receptive understanding and expressive use of vocabulary related to musical instruments.

accordion	banjo	bass drum
beat	blow	bongos
bow	cello	clarinet

Unit 15
Blooming Category Activities — Copyright © 2006 LinguiSystems, Inc.

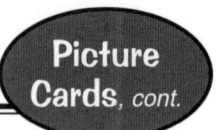

Musical Instruments

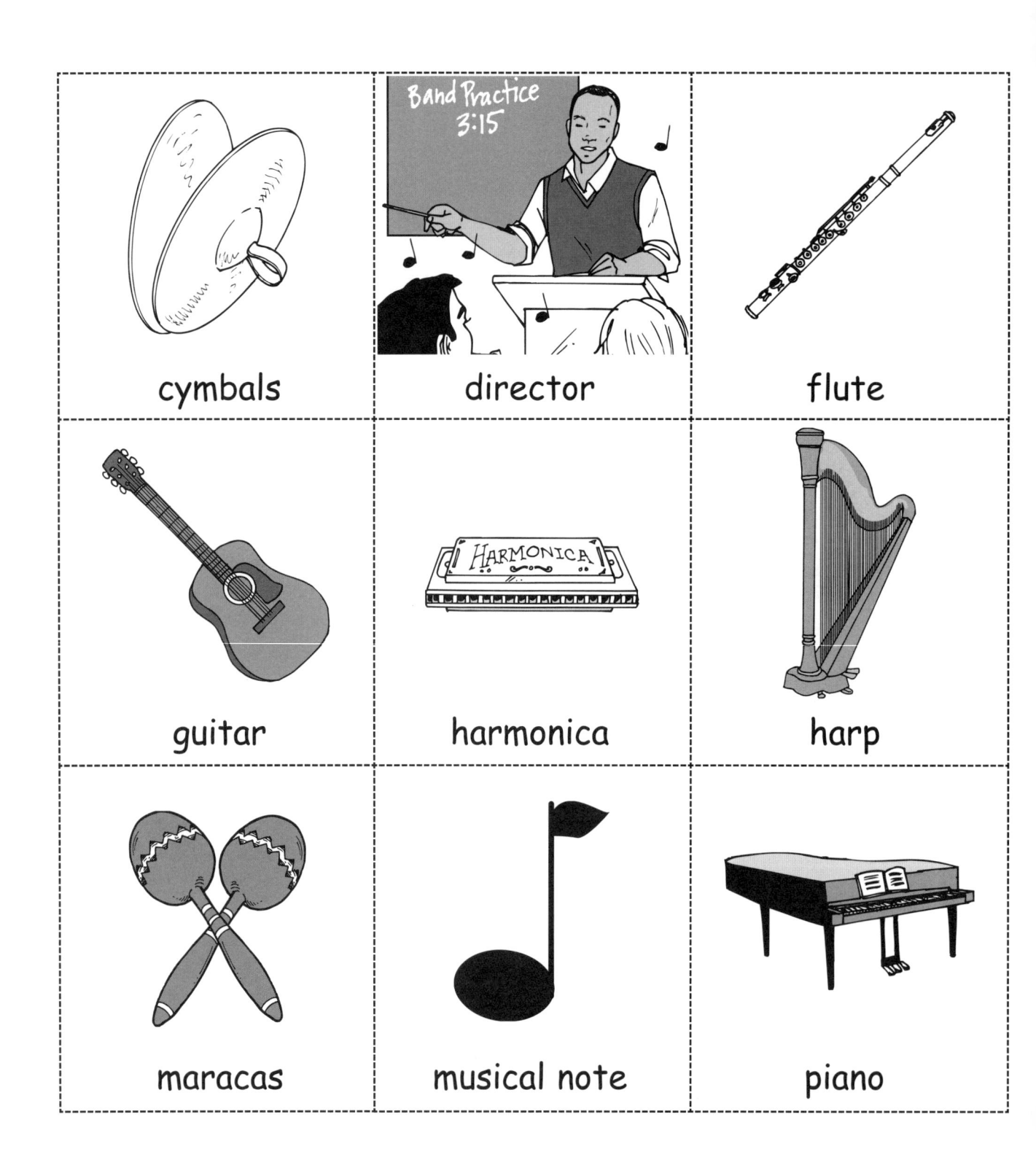

Picture Cards, cont.

cymbals	director	flute
guitar	harmonica	harp
maracas	musical note	piano

Unit 15
Blooming Category Activities

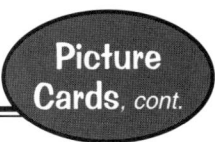

Musical Instruments

Picture Cards, cont.

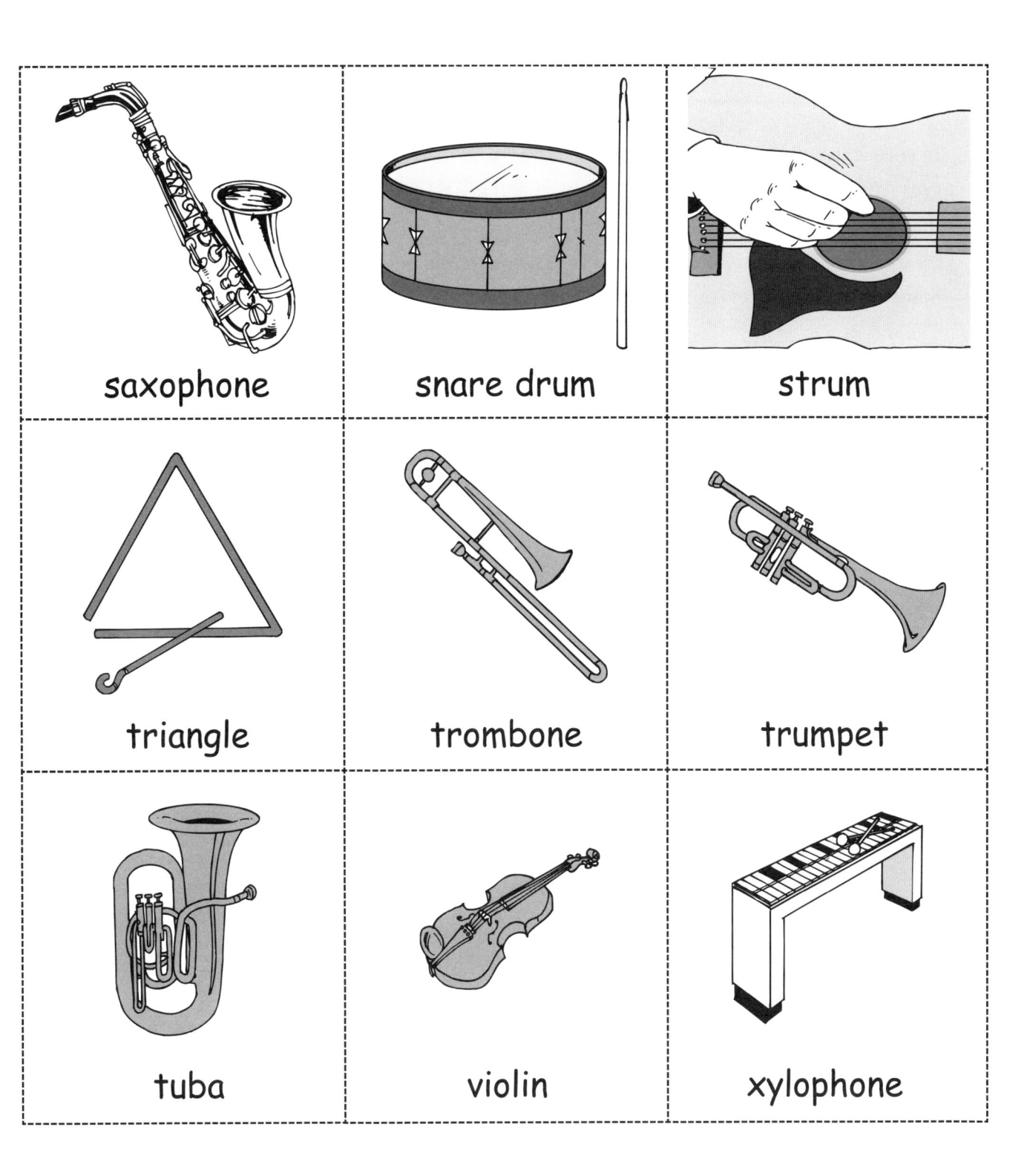

saxophone	snare drum	strum
triangle	trombone	trumpet
tuba	violin	xylophone

Unit 15
Blooming Category Activities

Musical Instruments

Family Letter

Dear Family,

In speech, we are learning about music and musical instruments and the vocabulary that goes with this category. You can help your child use this vocabulary at home. Talk about the picture below with your child and help her answer the questions. Then put this page up somewhere in your home to remind everyone to use musical vocabulary with your child. Some suggestions to encourage this are included at the bottom of this page.

Thank you, _____

Name the instruments in the band. Which one would you like to play?

- You need **drumsticks** to play a **drum**.
- She clanged the **cymbals** together at the end of the song.
- It's time to go to your **piano** lesson.
- I want a **guitar** for my birthday.
- The **conductor directed** the **orchestra**.
- We went on a field trip to hear an **orchestra**.
- I am learning to play a **harmonica**.
- The **band** marched in the **parade**.
- That **music** was too loud.
- Dad's CD has **banjo music** on it.

Unit 15
Blooming Category Activities

Musical Instruments

Activities

For some of these activities, you will photocopy and cut apart the picture cards on pages 161-163.

- Turn a tambourine upside down and put the picture cards in it. Let one child choose a picture and act out playing the instrument. Have the other children guess the instrument and use a sentence to tell how it is played.

- Listen to music on a CD. Have the children find picture cards to match the instruments they hear.

- Make a drum by covering and decorating an oatmeal box. As the child plays the drum, talk about different kinds of drums, using words like *loud*, *soft*, *slow*, and *fast*.

- Sort the musical instrument picture cards by those played with your hands and those played by blowing into them.

- Sort the musical instrument picture cards by those with strings and those without strings.

- Bring in real instruments or photographs of instruments. Have the children describe them by size, shape, color, texture, parts, and functions.

- Give the children kazoos, and let them take turns playing in or directing a "kazoo band." Talk about all of the instruments you would find in a marching band or a rock band.

- Tape the picture cards on the floor in a large circle. Play music from a tape, CD, or radio. Have the children march around the circle as in "Musical Chairs." When the music stops, have each child name the picture she has stopped on and name one of its parts.

- Look at real instruments or at pictures of instruments. Have the child count the parts of each instrument, such as the number of strings on a guitar, the number of keys on a keyboard, or the number of openings on a flute.

- Let each child make a tambourine using two paper plates, large dried beans, a stapler, and crayons or markers. Talk about the materials you use and the steps you take to make the tambourine. Then let the children play their tambourines, keeping the beat with some recorded music.

- Have each child talk about an instrument that she or a family member can play.

- Make maracas using small balloons, beans, craft sticks, and papier-mâché. Put a bean into a balloon. Blow up the balloon and tie it. Insert a craft stick in the end of the balloon. Cover the balloon with papier-mâché, and let it dry. Then stick a pin through the papier-mâché to pop the balloon inside. Have the child paint the maracas. Then let the child shake them, and talk about other instruments she could play by shaking them.

- Play a recording of classical music and let the children pretend to be the directors. Talk about the instruments in the orchestra and how to keep the beat of the music.

Musical Instruments

Worksheet

Objective: The child will increase vocabulary related to musical instruments by matching pictures of instruments and pictures of items used to play them.

Directions:
- Make photocopies of this page and page 167 for each child.
- Cut out the musical instruments at the bottom of this page.
- Name the pictures in the circles, and talk about which items are used to play each instrument.
- Have the child glue the pictures of the musical instruments in the circles they go with. Some circles will have more than one instrument.
- Let her choose one of the instruments and act out how she would play it.
- Encourage use of verbs such as *strum*, *blow*, and *beat*.

Unit 15
Blooming Category Activities
Copyright © 2006 LinguiSystems, Inc.

Worksheet, *cont.*

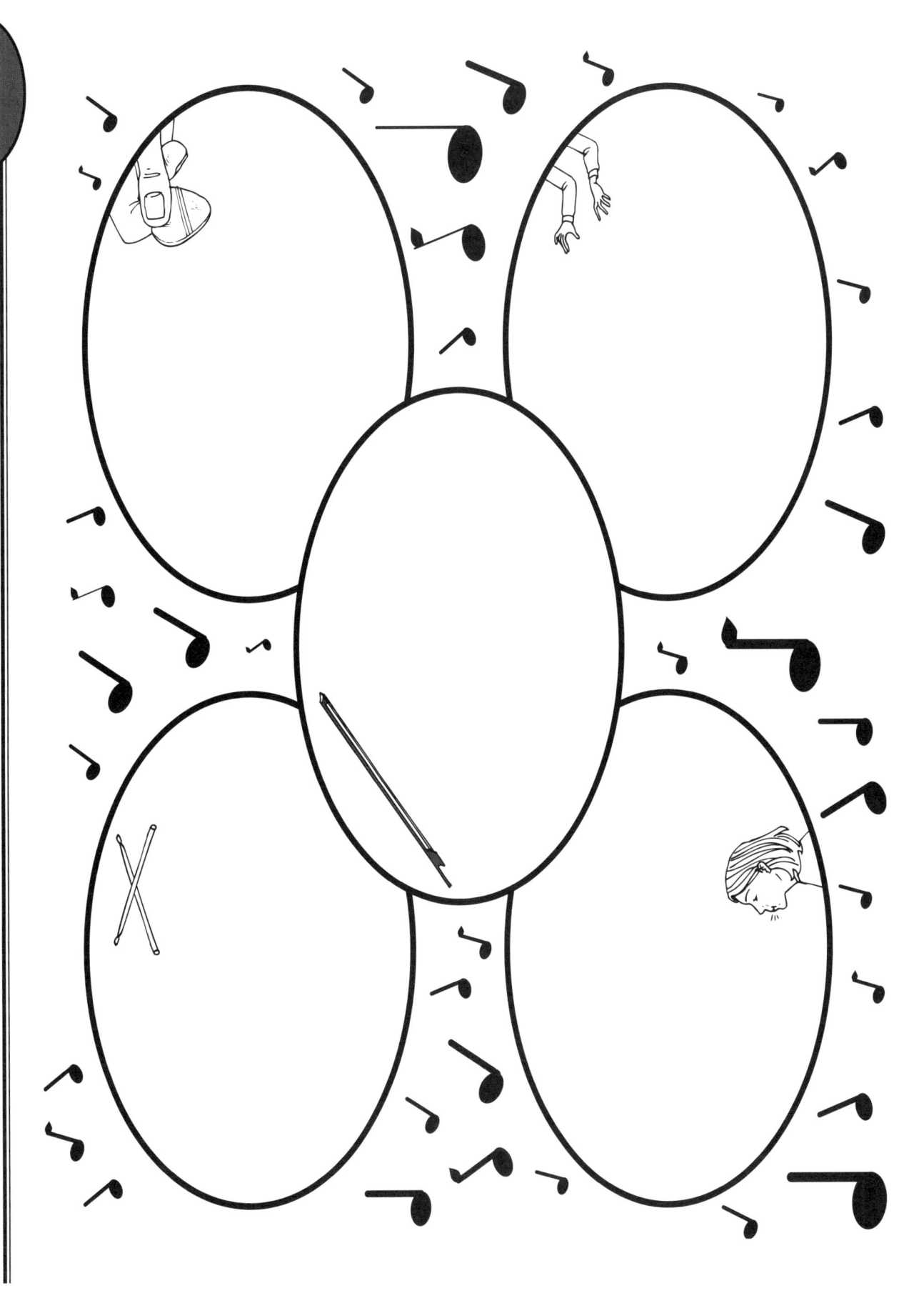

Musical Instruments

Unit 15
Blooming Category Activities — 167 — Copyright © 2006 LinguiSystems, Inc.

Musical Instruments

Concepts

⇒ **Objective**: The child will demonstrate receptive understanding and expressive use of basic concepts while completing the activity.

Marching to the Music

Materials:
- toy instruments, real instruments, or pretend instruments made from pots, pans, spoons, oatmeal boxes, etc.

Directions:
- Let each child choose an instrument, choose objects to make sound with, or decide on an instrument to pretend to play.
- Have the children follow the teacher's directions to form a marching band.
- Let the children take turns being the director.

Suggested Concepts to Target:

- **front/back**

  The horns go in **front** of the line.
  The drum goes in the **back**.

- **forward/backward**

  March three steps **forward**.
  Take one step **backward**.

- **loud/soft**

  The trumpet is too **loud**.
  I like the **soft** music.

- **first/middle/last**

  The **first** song was the best one.
  He is in the **middle** of the line.
  This is the **last** note.

- **all/some/none**

  All of us have instruments.
  Some of the music is pretty.
  None of us has a banjo.

- **always/sometimes/never**

  Our school's band **always** has a drummer.
  Sometimes band members wear uniforms.
  I have **never** played a harp.

- **before/after**

  Let's practice our song **before** we start marching.
  After I say "go," you can start marching.

- **in/on**

  Put the sheet music **in** your folder.
  Your fingers go **on** the keys.

Musical Instruments

Bloom's Taxonomy

Objective: The child will answer increasingly more difficult questions about musical instruments based on *Bloom's Taxonomy of Educational Objectives*.

Ask these questions while making and playing the Water Glass Xylophone on page 160 and throughout all of the activities in this lesson.

Knowledge
- Name the instrument we made with the glasses and water.
- How many glasses did we use to make the xylophone?
- What did we put in the glasses?
- What instrument do you strum with a pick?

Comprehension
- Tell how we made the xylophone.
- Compare the amount of water in each glass.
- Explain how you play a harp.
- Give an example of an instrument with strings.

Application
- Besides a trumpet, name some other instruments you play by blowing into them.
- What's another word for *loud*?
- How could you protect your ears from music that is too loud?
- Tell about an instrument you can play.

Analysis
- You use a pick to play a guitar. You use a bow to play a _____.
- What is the opposite of *soft music*?
- How are a violin and a cello alike?
- How are a piano and a banjo different?

Synthesis
- Create a new musical instrument.
- Suppose you lost your drumsticks. How could you play the drums?
- Compose a new song.
- What would it be like if you were in a rock band?

Evaluation
- Rank these instruments from softest to loudest: flute, drums, piano.
- What is your favorite musical instrument? Why?
- Would you rather play in a marching band or an orchestra? Why?

Seasons and Weather

Project

Weather Mobile

Materials:
- coat hanger
- yarn or string cut into 8" to 16" lengths
- crayons or markers
- scissors
- hole punch
- weather pictures on page 171

Directions:
- Make a copy of the weather pictures on page 171 for each child.
- Have the child color and cut out the pictures.
- Let the child name each weather-related object and talk about the season when that type of weather would occur. Encourage the child to use adjectives as he talks.
- Punch a hole in each picture.
- Tie a piece of yarn (string) through the hole.
- Tie the other end of the yarn (string) to the coat hanger.

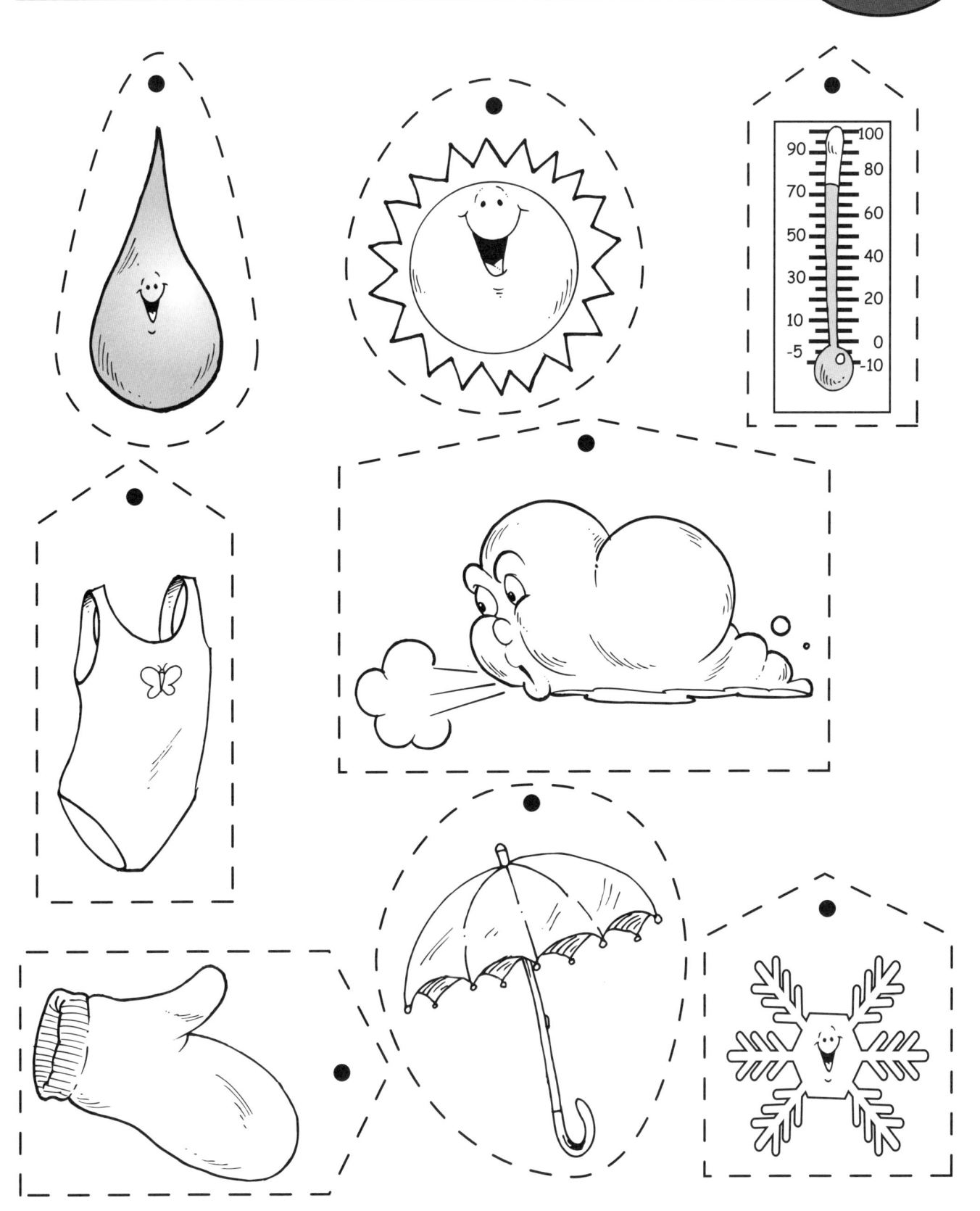

Seasons and Weather

Project, *cont.*

Unit 16
Blooming Category Activities

Seasons and Weather

Picture Cards

▶ **Objective:** The child will increase receptive understanding and expressive use of weather and seasonal vocabulary.

blizzard	clouds	fall
freezing	hail	harvest
hibernate	icicle	leaves

Unit 16
Blooming Category Activities

Copyright © 2006 LinguiSystems, Inc.

Seasons and Weather

Picture Cards, *cont.*

lightning	plant	puddle
rain	rainbow	sled
snowman	spring	summer

Unit 16
Blooming Category Activities — 173 — Copyright © 2006 LinguiSystems, Inc.

Seasons and Weather

Picture Cards, cont.

sunglasses	sunscreen	sunshine
sweating	thermometer	umbrella
weather	windy	winter

Seasons and Weather

Family Letter

Dear Family,

In speech, we are learning about weather and the seasons and the vocabulary that goes with this category. You can help your child practice this vocabulary at home. Talk about the picture below with your child and help him use season and weather words to answer the questions. Then put this page in a high traffic area in your home to remind everyone to help your child talk about the seasons and weather. Some ideas to encourage this are listed at the bottom of the page. Thank you, _____

What type of weather is this? What do you do when it is raining?

- We built a **snowman**.
- After the **rain** ended, there was a **rainbow**.
- The **wind blew** the **clouds** across the **sky**.
- Be sure to wear your **sunscreen**.
- The farmer had to **harvest** the crops.
- School was cancelled because of the **blizzard**.
- Mom forgot her **umbrella**.
- The **hail** dented the cars.
- **Thunder** can be loud.
- The **sun** went behind the **clouds**.

Seasons and Weather

Activities

For some of these activities, you will photocopy and cut apart the picture cards on pages 172-174.

- Let the child act out different seasonal activities. Have him describe what he's doing by using verbs such as *jump, splash, swim, run, fly,* and *shiver*.

- Sing weather-related songs with the children, such as "Itsy Bitsy Spider" or "Rain, Rain, Go Away." Act out the songs or do appropriate finger plays.

- Let the child dress a doll for different types of weather. Have him name each clothing item and tell what type of weather he would wear it in.

- Put the picture cards into a bag. Have the child pull out cards, name the pictures, and sort them according to seasons.

- Select a picture card. Have the child use various adjectives to tell about the picture.

- Put the weather pictures on the floor. Let the child toss a beanbag onto a picture. Then have the child name the weather and tell what type of clothes he would wear in that weather.

- Divide a large sheet of construction paper into three sections. Put a sun on one section, a raindrop on one section, and a snowflake on one section. Put all the picture cards in a pile and have the child select a picture. Then let him name the picture, tell what type of weather it relates to, and glue the picture on the appropriate section.

- Read a book about different types of weather or seasons. After each page, ask the child a question about the page that is related to weather or a season.

- Have the child cut out pictures from magazines that relate to weather or seasons. Let him talk about the pictures and glue them to a large sheet of construction paper or poster board to create a collage.

- Put seasonal objects such as *seashells, flowers, sand, grass,* and *seeds* in a shoebox. Have the child pull an object out of the box, making sure the other children don't see it. Have him describe the object using shape, size, color, and texture adjectives. Then let the other children guess what the object is.

- Draw a tree trunk on a brown sheet of construction paper. Then cut out leaves from different-colored construction paper. Have the child think of fall items or activities. Write each item or activity on a leaf and let the child glue the leaf to the tree.

Seasons and Weather

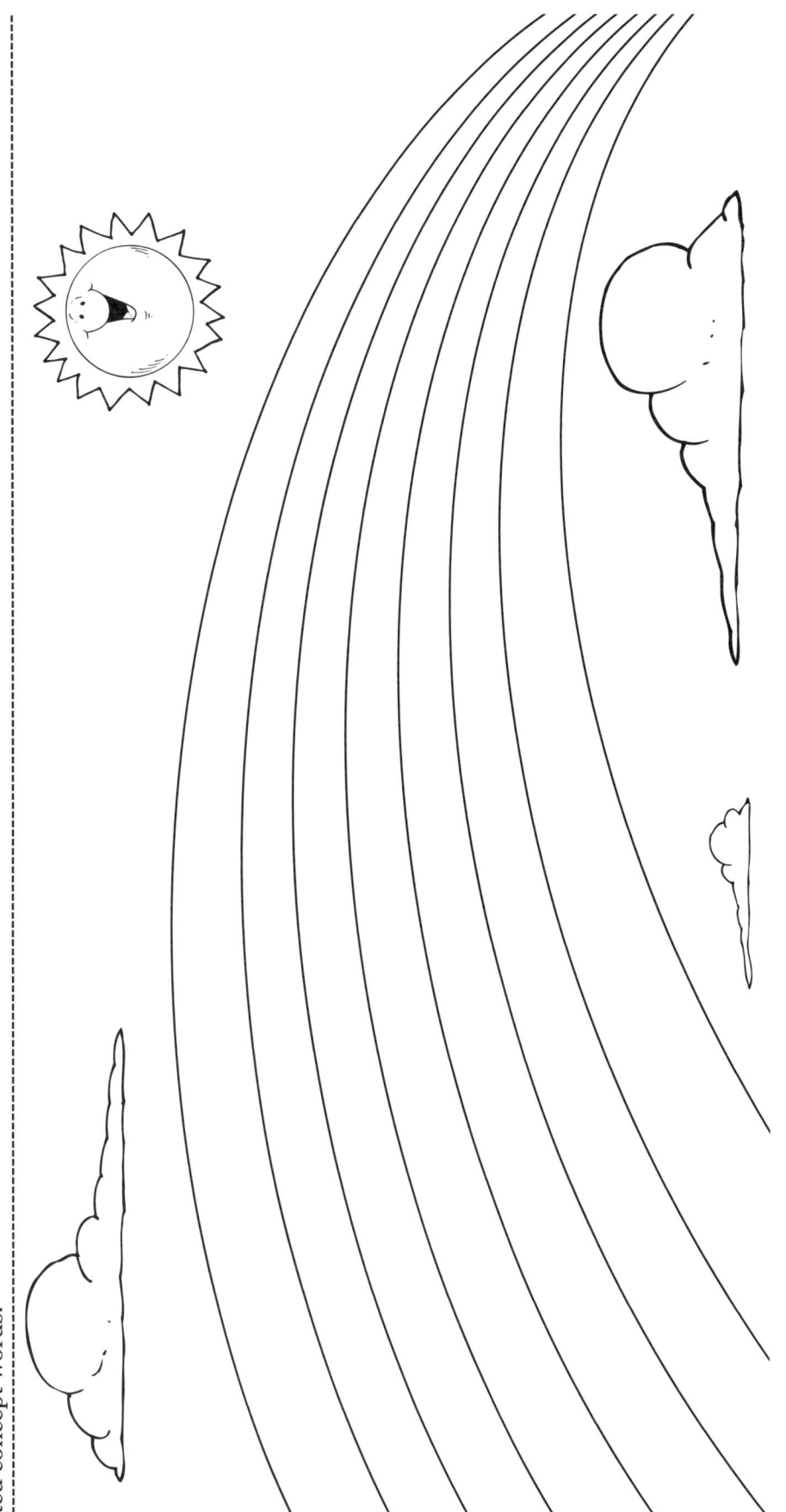

Worksheet

➤ **Objective:** The child will increase his receptive knowledge and expressive use of colors.

Photocopy the rainbow on this page for each child. If you want to work on receptive tasks, tell the child which crayon to select. Then tell him which band of the rainbow to color using concepts such as *top, bottom, first, middle, last, above,* and *below*. If you want to work on expressive tasks, let the child choose a crayon and tell its color. Then have him tell which band he colors using the previously listed concept words.

Unit 16
Blooming Category Activities

177

Copyright © 2006 LinguiSystems, Inc.

Seasons and Weather

Concepts

➡ **Objective**: The child will demonstrate receptive understanding and expressive use of basic concepts while completing the activity.

Cotton Ball Cloud

Materials:
- a small empty box, such as a pudding box or raisin box
- cotton balls
- glue
- yellow construction paper
- scissors

Directions:
- Have the child cut out a sun from the yellow construction paper.
- Let him glue cotton balls on the box to make a cloud. Tell him where to glue the cotton balls, using concepts such as *over, under, next to, beside, above*, and *below*. Use quantity concepts also to help with counting skills (i.e., "Glue two cotton balls on top of the box").
- When the box is covered with cotton balls, have the child hold the sun and the "cloud" like they are in the sky. Then instruct him to move them, using concepts such as *near, far, in front of, behind, over*, and *under*.

Suggested Concepts to Target:

- **over/under**
  Glue two cotton balls **over** the first one.
  The cloud is **under** the sun.

- **front/back**
  I see the name on the **front** of the box.
  The **back** of the box is covered with cotton balls.

- **top/middle/bottom**
  Tape the **top** of the box shut.
  The **middle** of the box does not have any cotton balls.
  I put the cotton ball on the **bottom**.

- **next to/beside**
  Put your cloud **next to** mine.
  Move the sun **beside** the cloud.

- **far/near**
  Put the sun **far** away from the cloud.
  The cotton balls are **near** each other.

- **in/on**
  There is nothing **in** the box.
  I put lots of cotton balls **on** the box.

- **left/right**
  Can you move the sun to the **left**?
  The sun is on the **right** side of the cloud.

Seasons and Weather

Bloom's Taxonomy

Objective: The child will answer increasingly more difficult questions about seasons and weather based on *Bloom's Taxonomy of Educational Objectives*.

Ask these questions while doing the Weather Mobile activity on page 170 and throughout all of the activities in this lesson.

Knowledge
- Name the weather pictures we used on the mobile.
- How many items were on the mobile?
- What did we use to make the mobile?
- Where do you see lightning?

Comprehension
- Describe what the sky looks like when it is going to storm.
- Draw a picture of a fall day.
- Compare a tree in summer and one in winter.
- Explain how you made your mobile.

Application
- Tell which items on the mobile are related to nice weather and which are related to bad weather.
- Name some other weather items you could put on your mobile.
- Tell how you can get leaves off your yard.
- What is another word for *autumn*?

Analysis
- Hot is to summer as cold is to _____.
- How are thunder and lightning alike?
- How are the sun and a cloud different?
- Compare your mobile to your friends' mobiles.

Synthesis
- Design a new umbrella.
- What would it be like if it snowed a lot and you did not have a shovel?
- Think of different materials we could use to make the mobile.
- How can you get cool in the summer besides using a fan?

Evaluation
- What is your favorite type of weather? Why?
- Would you rather use a blanket or a coat to get warm? Why?
- If it was raining and all you had to keep dry was a trash bag, would that work? Why?

Bugs and Insects

Project

Paper Plate Ladybug

Materials:
- two red paper plates
- black construction paper
- one brad
- scissors
- glue
- "wiggly eyes"

Directions:
- Cut one paper plate in half to form two wings.
- Have the child cut out circles from the black construction paper to make ladybug spots.
- Let the child glue the spots onto the wings. Tell the child where to glue the spots using concepts such as *next to, above, over, left,* and *right*.
- After the child glues all the spots on the wings, have her count the spots.
- Put the two wings on top of the other paper plate. Punch one hole through both plates, put the brad through the hole, and secure. Open and close the wings.
- Cut a head out of the black construction paper and glue it near the brad.
- Glue two eyes on the ladybug's head.

Bugs and Insects

Picture Cards

Objective: The child will increase receptive understanding and expressive use of bugs and insects vocabulary.

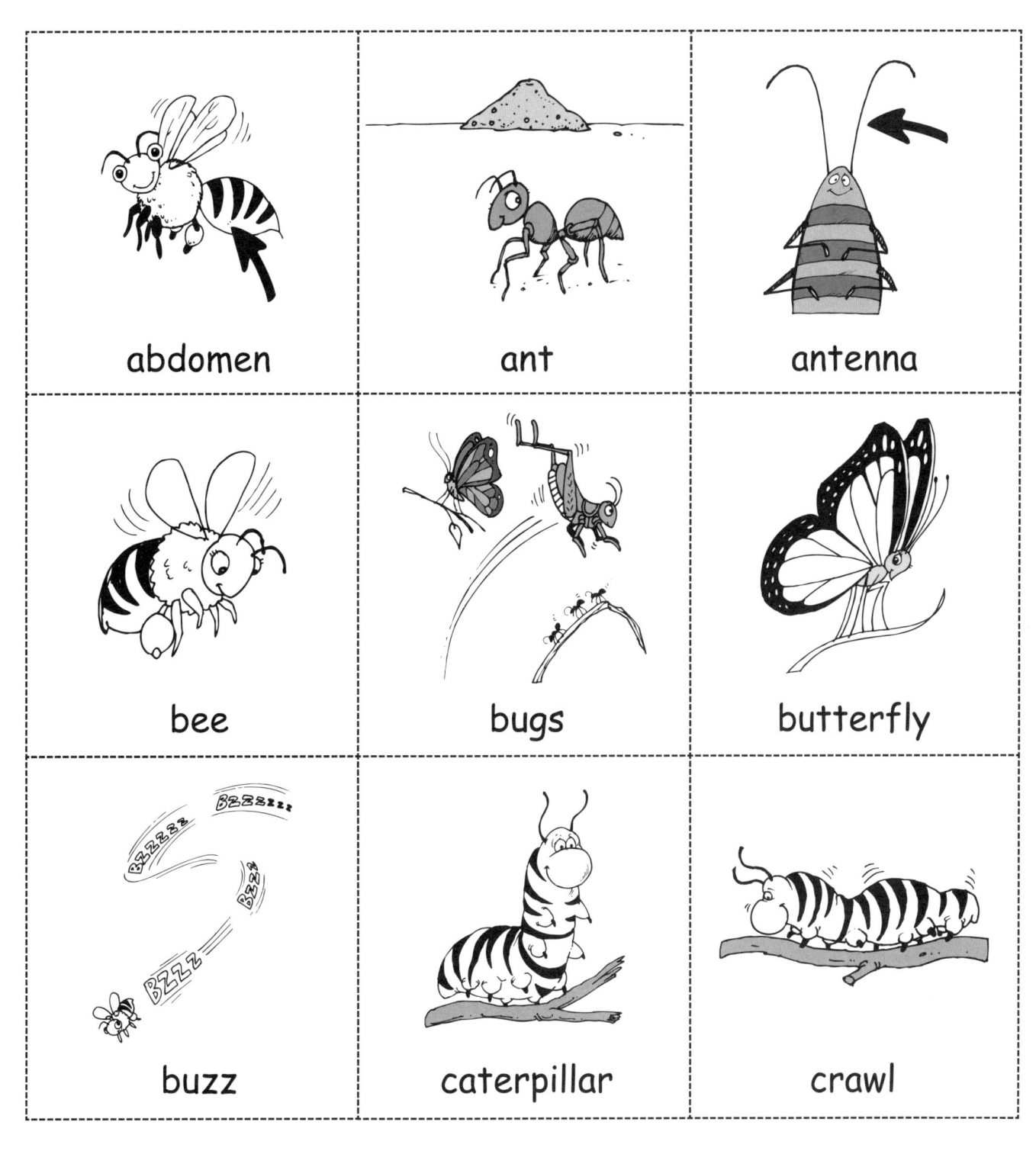

abdomen	ant	antenna
bee	bugs	butterfly
buzz	caterpillar	crawl

Unit 17
Blooming Category Activities
181
Copyright © 2006 LinguiSystems, Inc.

Bugs and Insects

Picture Cards, cont.

cricket	dragonfly	fly
grasshopper	head	hop
ladybug	legs	lightning bug

Unit 17
Blooming Category Activities

Bugs and Insects

Picture Cards, cont.

mosquito	moth	praying mantis
spider	sting	stinger
thorax	wasp	wing

Bugs and Insects

Family Letter

Dear Family,

In speech, we are learning about bugs and insects and the vocabulary that goes with this category. You can help your child practice this vocabulary at home. Talk about the picture below with your child and help her use bug and insect words to answer the questions. Then put this page in a high traffic area in your home to remind everyone to help your child talk about bugs and insects. Some ideas to encourage this are listed at the bottom of the page.

Thank you, _____

Have you ever seen an insect display at a zoo? Which insects had stingers?

- The **bee** can **fly** into the flower.
- The **grasshopper hopped** by the dog.
- A **spider** has **eight legs**.
- Can you tell me the names of some **insects**?
- Our class watched the **caterpillar** turn into a **butterfly**.

- The **bee's stinger** is in its **abdomen**.
- The **butterfly's antennae** are on its **head**.
- I saw a **caterpillar crawl** on the leaf.
- A **mosquito** can **bite** you.
- He put the **bugs** into a jar.

Unit 17
Blooming Category Activities

Bugs and Insects — Activities

For some of these activities, you will photocopy and cut apart the picture cards on pages 181-183.

- Sing children's songs or do finger plays about bugs, such as the *Itsy Bitsy Spider*, *The Ants Go Marching In*, and *Little Miss Muffet*.

- Place the picture cards of the various bugs and insects around the room. Give the child a fly swatter. Have her name the bug and then swat it.

- Bury the picture cards in a large container filled with sand or dirt. Give the child a shovel and let her dig for bugs. Once she finds a picture card, have her name the picture.

- Cut out pictures of bugs and insects from magazines and create a collage. Have the child name the bugs and also tell about their body parts. The child can also compare the bugs and talk about how they are the same and how they are different, using size, color, and shape adjectives.

- Draw a garden scene on a large sheet of construction paper or poster board. Have the child choose a picture card. Tell her where to put it using a variety of concepts, such as *over the flower*, *in the dirt*, *next to the tree*, and *above the bird*.

- Create a spider web using a ball of yarn. Have one child name an insect or insect body part and then roll the ball of yarn to another child. The child that gets the ball of yarn names an insect or insect body part, then holds onto the yarn as she rolls the ball to a new child. Repeat this process until all the yarn is gone and the children have created a large spider web.

- Make a spider from an egg carton. Cut the sectioned part of an egg carton in half lengthwise. Then cut it again so you have four sections of the egg carton. Punch four holes on each side for the legs. Cut four pipe cleaners to six-inch lengths. These will be the spider's legs. Have the child put a pipe cleaner in one hole and through the hole on the other side. After the legs are on, have the child count how many legs her spider has.

- Draw three bug bodies out of red, blue, and green construction paper. Punch three holes into each side of these bug bodies. Cut three red, three blue, and three green pipe cleaners in half. These will be the bugs' legs. Put the pipe cleaners in a bag. Have the child pull out a pipe cleaner, name the color, and match the pipe cleaner to the same-colored paper bug. Let the child attach the leg to the body.

- Bring in an encyclopedia or picture book about bugs and insects. Have the child match the picture cards to the pictures in the book.

- Let each child catch a bug or insect at home and bring it to school in a jar, or have them draw a picture of a bug they have seen. Then let each child tell about her bug.

Bugs and Insects

Worksheet

> **Objective:** The child will demonstrate receptive understanding and expressive use of vocabulary associated with bugs and insects.

Directions:
- Make photocopies of this page and page 187 for each child.
- Have the child color each bug, following directions such as *Color the grasshopper green*, *Color the ant blue*, *Use three different colors for the butterfly's wings*, and *Make the butterfly's antennae brown*. Be certain that you use all colors to help the child increase her knowledge of colors.
- After the child colors all the bugs, ask her questions that she can answer to demonstrate expressive knowledge, such as "What color is the butterfly's antenna?" and "What colors did you use on the butterfly's wings?"
- Ask the child, "How does the _____ move?" The child answers and then glues the bug in the appropriate column on page 187.

Unit 17
Blooming Category Activities

Copyright © 2006 LinguiSystems, Inc.

Bugs and Insects

Worksheet, *cont.*

How Does the Bug Move?

Crawl	Fly	Hop

Bugs and Insects

Concepts

Objective: The child will demonstrate receptive understanding and expressive use of basic concepts while completing the activity.

How Does Your Garden Grow?

Materials:
- flower garden scene on page 189
- bug pictures on page 186
- scissors
- crayons
- glue

Directions:
- Make photocopies of the garden picture on page 189 and the bug pictures on page 186 for each child.
- Have the child color the bugs and cut them apart.
- Tell the child where to glue a picture (receptive) or let the child glue the bug on the garden scene and tell where she glued it (expressive).

Suggested Concepts to Target:

• **over/under**	Glue the butterfly **over** a flower. Put the cricket **under** a flower.
• **in/on**	Draw the sun **in** the sky. Glue the ant **on** the path.
• **next to/beside**	Glue the spider **next to** a flower. Put the bee **beside** a flower.
• **left/right**	Find a leaf on the **left** side of the picture and glue the caterpillar on it. Put the mosquito on the child's **right** arm.
• **same/different**	How is the bee the **same** as the butterfly? How is the ant **different** from the caterpillar?
• **first/last**	What did you glue on **first**? What did you color **last**?

Bugs and Insects

Concepts, cont.

Unit 17
Blooming Category Activities — 189 — Copyright © 2006 LinguiSystems, Inc.

Bugs and Insects

Bloom's Taxonomy

Objective: The child will answer increasingly more difficult questions about bugs and insects based on *Bloom's Taxonomy of Educational Objectives*.

Ask these questions while doing the Paper Plate Ladybug activity on page 180 and throughout all of the activities in this lesson.

Knowledge
- How many spots does your ladybug have?
- Where did you glue the head?
- What did we use to make the spots?
- Where do you find ladybugs?

Comprehension
- Tell how you made your ladybug.
- What is another bug that has spots?
- Draw a picture of another type of bug.
- Describe how you made the ladybug's wings.

Application
- What is another word for *insect*?
- What would happen if a bug did not have wings?
- Name another insect that has six legs.
- What else could you have used to make the ladybug's spots?

Analysis
- How are an ant and a ladybug alike?
- Why did we use two paper plates?
- What did you do first when you made the ladybug?
- A frog jumps and a ladybug _____.

Synthesis
- Tell me all the ways a ladybug can move.
- What would it be like if you could fly?
- What would happen if a ladybug lost one wing?
- How else could we have made the spots stick to the ladybug's wings?

Evaluation
- Which bug do you like best? Why?
- Would it work to keep a bug in a jar? Why?
- Would it be better to use black markers or black felt to make the ladybug's spots? Why?